Orchid

The Fatal Attraction

Orchid

The Fatal Attraction

Dr Anne Ronse

Photography
Bart Van Leuven
Tom Swijns

stichting
kunstboek

Introduction

Orchids are born seducers. Their flowers are designed to entice insects so that they take pollen from one flower to another, thereby ensuring sexual reproduction. Orchids achieve this through all sorts of tricks in which the pollinators are sometimes rewarded, but often end up being deceived.

Human beings are also seduced by the beauty of these striking flowers. Although the basic structure is always the same, orchid flowers are extremely diverse, not only in shape but also in scent and colour. Soft pastel shades or vivid hues, contrasting and flashy colours or alarming, dark creations — from bizarre and intricate constructions to beautifully simple outlines, orchids have it all. It is therefore not surprising that they have appealed to the human imagination throughout history. In ancient times, only a few species were known in the West because most orchids originate from tropical regions. It was especially in the period after the discovery of America and during the Colonial period that knowledge of orchids increased considerably. Their refined beauty seduced people, stimulated their imagination, and caused passions to run high. Some collectors were (and still are) prepared to pay a fortune for orchids. In the days when travelling to distant countries was a very dangerous undertaking, many orchid hunters perished in the jungle whilst trying to seize possession of some rare species and bring it back to Europe. Nowadays, unfortunately, there are still people who illegally search for orchids in inaccessible areas to smuggle them over borders, despite international legislation to protect them. Even with decades of plunder, new species are still being discovered on a regular basis.

This book is divided into two parts.

The first part tells the story of the discovery of orchids throughout history and describes the way in which people experience orchids and the impression these plants have made on humanity. In the East, there is an emphasis on positive qualities, such as grace and grandeur. In the West, orchids have been seen mainly as a symbol of reproduction and sexuality. In certain periods, they were associated with negative qualities, often related to extravagance and sex.

In the second part, orchids are described more 'neutrally' in an attempt to divorce them from human interpretation. The design and structure of their flowers are put into a functional context. In other words, we ask questions such as: Why are orchids the way they are? What is the purpose of those amazingly intricate shapes? Why these marvellous colours? Why that awful smell from some, and heavenly scents from others? The answers to these questions are usually found in their reproduction mechanisms. After all, like all flowers, these are sexual organs whose purpose is to ensure the survival of their species.

I Orchids throughout history
the story of their discovery

The Far East: grace and grandeur   10

The Ancient World: testicle plants and ice cream   14

The great discoveries   18
· Tropical orchids > 18
· Orchid mania > 21
· Myriads of orchids > 22

Orchid hunter: a dangerous profession   26

Bitter competition and rivalry   34

Parasites? No, epiphytes!   36

Vanilla   40

Orchids with a genealogy   42

From exclusive collector's item to everyday domestic plant   46

Orchid fever: orchid maniacs and smugglers   52

Orchids in art and literature   60

Orchids between heaven and earth   66

II

Orchids as seducers
a story of seduction

Everything you ever wanted to know about orchid sex   72

Charles Darwin and the Theory of Evolution   78

A bee in the bonnet   82

Crocodiles, antelopes, octopuses and invisible colours   90

A gross deception   96

Orchids down under   100

Transsexuals and drunken bees (Catasetinae and Stanhopeinae)   104

Dracula and other horror stories   110

Slipper orchids and slippery customers   118

Tiny jewels   126

Rotting elephants and mobiles   130

Butterflies and hummingbirds   134

Glossary of terms   142

Literature   143

I

Orchids throughout history
the story of their discovery

The Far East:
grace and grandeur

For thousands of years, orchids have been appreciated in China, not only for the beauty of the flowers, but also for their often delightful aromas, and elegance of their leaves. Orchids are described in herbal medicine books over three thousand years old. The first person to mention them was Sheng Nun, a Chinese emperor who gave advice about how to use a species of *Dendrobium*. Around 300 B.C., two species of orchids were described in the first manuscript dedicated entirely to botany, which was written by the minister Ki-Han.

The Chinese were not only interested in the medicinal properties of orchids. They regarded orchids as a symbol of elegance, refinement, grandeur, purity and spiritual perfection. Orchids were included in the I Ching, the centuries old 'Book of Changes' which dates back to the first millennium B.C. This book contains poetic texts with strong symbolism, used for fortune telling over thousands of years. You simply open the book and the text which catches your eye randomly provides you with answers to the questions occupying your mind. One of the texts states that "When two beings are united in the intimacy of their hearts, their words are sweet and powerful like the perfume of orchids".

Orchids have been called the kings of aromatic plants. The oldest known Chinese dictionary, Shuowen (second century A.D.) defines 'lan' as a perfumed plant but was particularly associated with orchids, Cymbidiums in particular. The great Chinese philosopher Confucius (551 to 479 B. C.) wrote that associating with good people is comparable to the experience of entering a room filled with 'lan'. In the end, you don't smell the fragrance anymore, but you are touched and changed by it on the inside. Another passage written by Confucius states: "Although the 'lan' grow in deep forests, they never withhold their heavenly fragrance, even if there is no one around to smell it."

In many parts of the world, Cymbidiums are known mainly as cut flowers, originating from cultivars with large, colourful flowers. There are, however, some fifty species, most of which grow in the wild in Asia. The wild species have smaller flowers with less striking colours, and long leaves which tend to look like grass and are extremely graceful. The flowers of numerous varieties disperse a delightful scent said to be a refined combination of jasmine, lily of the valley and lemon peel. *Cymbidium linearisepalum*, for example, possesses a fascinating perfume in which separate 'tones' of jasmine, lily of the valley, apple blossom, and peach make up a perfectly harmonious whole.

From the tenth century onwards, wealthy Chinese began the practice of taking a flowering orchid with them on journeys so that they could enjoy the scent. Lo Chi, a governor from the Chinese Soeng dynasty (from 960 to 1279 A.D.), wrote: "I treat orchids as my most virtuous and honourable friends. In the morning, I am blessed by their perfume, whilst at night I enjoy their flowers. Together with my book and my wine, we read and drink together."

In the distant past, Chinese noblemen kept collections of Cymbidiums, and during the Wei dynasty (220 to 265 A.D.), this habit was adopted by the aristocracy. Orchids became part of the family property and were passed on to their heirs. In some families of Chinese orchid growers, plants have been passed down for over five hundred years from generation to generation. During the Tang dynasty (618 to 907 A.D.), nurseries became popular and orchids became affordable for the middle classes. Thanks to centuries of

Cymbidium cochleare a native of India and Sikkim has hanging >
inflorescences with interesting brownish coloured flowers.

cultivation and refinement, many cultivars (cultivated varieties) were created with specific colours or perfumes, and which are still present today in China and Japan. For example, there are many varieties of *Cymbidium sinense*, most of which have flowers from pure yellow to red, but some versions are almost black, and there is also a white version. One of these near-black varieties is 'Faichow Dark', which flowers around the Chinese New Year and whose dark purple flowers spread a sweet, aromatic scent. Other Cymbidiums are cultivated for their charming leaves, such as the 'Golden Threads Ponytail', a variety of *C. ensifolium* with long, thin variegated leaves which are beautifully yellow-veined.

From China, the cult of aromatic orchids spread to Japan. Here, orchids were called 'ran' and symbolised virtue, simplicity, charm, and feminine grace. Orchids grown in Japan

bore the name To-yo-ran, whilst the name Yo-ran was used for orchids which were imported from Western countries in later times. The To-yo-ran included species originating from Japan, China, Taiwan and Korea; these include numerous varieties of *Cymbidium*, but also *Sedirea japonica* and *Dendrobium moniliforme*. Each social class had a preference for a certain group or genus of orchids. The Japanese bushido warriors, better known as samurai, formed an educated martial elite involved in cultural affairs. They cultivated *Neofinetia falcata*, a white flowering orchid with a sweet perfume which smells like lily of the valley during the day and butter biscuits at night. The Japanese samurai used to take these particular orchids with them on their travels from their estates to the capital so that during the journey they could enjoy the beauty of the flowers and their delightful scent. The so-called Samurai Orchid was thought to symbolise the courage and

Cymbidium hybrid

endurance of this martial class. They set off in search of these plants on deserted and remote islands, facing all sorts of dangers and treacherous currents along the way. For a considerable period of time, those who did not belong to the samurai class were forbidden to possess such an orchid. The merchants and prosperous social classes preferred Cymbidiums. Meanwhile, the Imperial aristocracy and Imperial Household had a preference for 'Sekkoku, the orchid that lengthens the life of man' (*Dendrobium moniliforme*).

Today, certain orchids are still used in Japanese households for perfuming the 'style room' (*washitsu*) - they are placed in the *tokonoma*, an elevated alcove which forms the aesthetic centre of the room. Calligraphic parchment scrolls and Ikebana flower arrangements are displayed there, all in accordance with the traditional Japanese style.

It is mainly *Cymbidium faberi* and *C. kanran* which are used nowadays for this purpose, but others include the 'Imperial Sekkoku', the Samurai Orchid, and *Calanthe izu-insularis*, which give off a scent of pepper plants. Incidentally, the Japanese cosmetics giant Shiseido has developed a perfume based on orchids called Tentatrice (seducer) available only in Japan. It is a complicated mixture of jasmine and lily of the valley, with oak moss, musk and amber scent, combined with methyl jasmonate. The latter ingredient provides a warm, intoxicating feminine scent and the typical fragrance of Chinese Cymbidiums.

The Ancient World:
testicle plants
and ice cream

In Western history, the first known records of orchids date back to Theophrastus, a Greek philosopher who lived from 370 to 285 B.C. and who studied under Plato and Aristotle. He wrote the 'Historia Plantarum', a major work in ten volumes, effectively an encyclopaedia of all species of plants known at that time. Here he describes orchids under the name 'Orkhis', the Greek word for testicle. The book mentions the fact that these plants consist of two tubers in the shape of an olive, but with bigger dimensions, one of which is smooth and tough, whilst the other is wrinkled and softer. We now know that this describes the tuber formed during the current year, which is still hard, and the older tuber formed during the previous year. These tubers contain stored food for the plant in the same way as onions and daffodil bulbs. The species of the genus *Orchis* have passed on their name to the entire family of orchids (Orchidaceae), although only a small minority within this family actually possesses such bulb-shaped roots.

After Theophrastus, orchids were described by Dioscorides, a Greek scholar and surgeon in the Roman army during the first century A.D. He was both a physicist and botanist and wrote a significant work in five volumes, 'De Materia Medica', which became the predecessor of all pharmacopoeia. This book contained all known plant remedies and the (supposed) medical effects attributed to them by the Greeks, Romans, and other civilisations of that time. For a long time, it was the leading reference work on medicinal plants and was consulted frequently until at least the sixteenth century. It mentions a few orchids which existed in the region around the Mediterranean Sea, including the Green-winged Orchid (*Orchis morio*), which was one of the most common species in Western Europe 150 years ago.

The medicinal properties that have been attributed to orchids usually relate to the area of sexuality and reproduction. According to Dioscorides, the roots were cooked and eaten; in the case of men, they were supposed to determine the gender of their children, depending on whether the new or old tuber was eaten. For women, consuming the tubers was considered to affect their passion; the old tuber would strengthen it, whilst the young tuber would suppress it. Orchids were also supposed to possess aphrodisiacal properties for men. Up until the Middle Ages and the Renaissance, orchids were known by the generic term 'Satyrion', because eating their tubers was supposed to give men the strength and desires of satyrs. In the English herbal book 'Gerard's Herbal', written by John Gerard in 1597, an orchid was described as *Satyrion feminina*, "the food of satyrs that causes their excessive sexual behaviour". Ascribing such effects to these orchids perfectly fits the Doctrine of Signatures. This is an ancient medical theory first applied in China which says that everything in nature has been created by God and that the appearance of the plants themselves indicates the diseases for which they can be a remedy. If certain parts of plants resemble certain parts of the human body, they were supposed to have an effect on these parts.

In the seventeenth and eighteenth centuries, the idea arose that orchids sprout from the sperm of wild animals that mate in the mountains and meadows, or from the rotting cadavers of these animals. The Jesuit Athanasius Kircher described this in his book 'Mundus Subterraneus' (Amsterdam, 1664-1665). Kircher believed that the proof for his theory could be found in the resemblance of orchid flowers to some

The Lizard Orchid, **Himantoglossum hircinum**, > is the largest indigenous orchid of Western Europe.

If you look carefully, you may see a resemblance of a human figure in the flower of the Man Orchid (**Aceras anthropophorum**).

insects, such as flies, wasps, and bees. According to popular belief, these insects spontaneously originated from the rotting corpses of horses, cows, and other large animals. Various European orchids have flowers that resemble animals, such as the Monkey Orchid (*Orchis simia*), the Fly Orchid (*Ophrys insectifera*), and the Bee Orchid (*Ophrys apifera*). Species with broad, square flowers were said to originate from the sperm of bulls, whilst those with slimmer flowers were supposed to come from the sperm of stallions. In his book,

Kircher also provides an engraving of orchid flowers that resemble birds, 'Ornithomorpha', and others resembling human figures, such as 'Anthropomorpha'.

One of the most fascinating species depicted by Kircher is the Lizard Orchid (*Himantoglossum hircinum*). This is the largest of the orchids indigenous to Western Europe, growing up to almost one metre in height. The flowering of the Lizard Orchid is a phenomenal sight in regions such as the Dordogne in France, where they still grow in large quantities along the roads in some places. Each plant is adorned with twenty to thirty decorative flowers with long, curly petals that are greenish or reddish in colour. What is special about this orchid, however, is its strong smell, reminiscent of male goats, as the French name ('Orchis Bouc') indicates. However, it is also a sweet smell, with even a touch of vanilla. Due to its particular smell, bumblebees and honeybees avoid these flowers, although some beetles are attracted to them. Even a mosquito was once found with the pollen lumps of this species on its snout. The actual pollinator, however, is the *Andraena carbonaria*, a type of mining bee. Although the Lizard Orchid exists mainly around the Mediterranean Sea, it is also found as far away as Belgium and Great Britain. This species seems to have been progressing north in recent decades, possibly under the influence of the warming climate.

In the countries around the Mediterranean Sea, orchids are still regarded as aphrodisiacs. Several species are used to make a type of ice cream using a flour obtained from their tubers known as 'salep'. The word salep is derived from the Arabic word 'sahlab', which means 'fox testicles.' This ice cream is eaten mainly in Turkey, where it is estimated that about sixty million tubers are collected for the purpose each year. The most popular salep species are *Orchis mascula* (Early-purple Orchid), *Orchis anatolica* (Anatolian Orchid), *Dactylorhiza maculata* (Heath-spotted Orchid), and *Dactylorhiza majalis* (Broad-leaved Orchid). In order to make this ice cream, new tubers are excavated and subsequently washed and soaked in warm water for almost an hour so that they can be peeled. Then they are dried in the sun for a week, and then ground into flour. The salep is then mixed with milk and sugar and beaten into a cream using a metal rod. Salep ice cream is firm and therefore you have to eat it with a knife and fork. The elasticity from the processed tuber's mucilage means that it can be stretched out to make a skipping rope. This may not sound very appetising, but salep ice cream is enjoyed by many and available in many different flavours such as vanilla, pistachio, apricot and other fruits. In addition, it is believed to have healing properties - to increase male potency, cure poor souls who are love sick, prevent a humpback, cholera and tuberculosis, cure bronchitis, reduce labour pains, and stop hands and feet from shaking! In Greece and Syria, salep is added to a hot drink with cinnamon. In England it was brewed into a drink called 'saloop' that was especially popular until the first half of the nineteenth century.

Further south, some African ground orchids are also collected to be used in food. In Zambia, Malawi, and Katanga (the southern part of Congo), the equivalent of salep is called chikanda or kinaka. This is cooked mainly with the flour of groundnuts and sold as a delicacy. Both salep and chikanda are exported to Western Europe where they are used to prepare industrial ice cream because of its high mucilage content. In Tanzania, however, researchers from the University of Dar-es-Salaam have sounded the alarm bell because approximately eighty-five species of orchids are threatened with imminent extinction. These orchids are collected in the southern highlands and exported illegally to neighbouring Zambia. The illegal trade involves over two million orchids from the genera, *Disa, Satyrium, Habenaria*, and *Brachycorytis*. Unfortunately, the consumption of chikanda has strongly increased in recent years in Zambia, especially in urban regions, sending these plants closer to extinction.

In South Africa's Transvaal province, men of the Lobedu tribe traditionally chew the stem of Lissochilus and Eulophia orchids to obtain an erection, as a kind of 'Viagra'. According to Zulus, there are other orchids which would be effective for this purpose. Moreover, in order to seduce a lady, young men traditionally put a Leopard Orchid leaf, Ansellia africana, under their armpits; and a brew was made from the roots of this same species as an aphrodisiac. It had one more beneficial effect (at least, for some) because this brew was said to make unmarried ladies infertile for one night.

The great discoveries

Tropical orchids

In the ancient Western world, only a limited number of orchids were known because only a few hundred species grow in Europe and around the Mediterranean Sea. However, the discovery of the Americas and exploration of overseas colonies meant that the abundance of tropical and subtropical orchids was gradually discovered. The first tropical orchid grown in Europe was *Bletia verecunda*, a species from the Bahamas. This plant was cultivated in 1731 by an Englishman, Mr. Wager. It was in England that the strongest interest in orchids was developing, and Britain later became the most important centre for orchid cultivation. From the seventeenth century onwards, increasing numbers of tropical orchids were imported into Europe, either alive or in dried form as her-

baria, and consequently more and more species were described by botanists. Even William Bligh, the infamous captain of the Bounty, brought a new species of orchid (*Dendrobium linguiforme*) back from Australia to Europe. The Bounty was a ship in the service of the British Navy, instructed to collect breadfruit trees from Tahiti and take them to America. However, in Tahiti some of the crew revolted and began a mutiny. The captain was left adrift in a small boat, together with eighteen other sailors, but he eventually managed to reach the island of Timor. This story has been depicted in several popular films, the first of which was 'The Wake of the Bounty' with actor Erroll Flynn in 1933; this was soon followed by a new version with Clark Gable in 1935. In 1962, 'Mutiny on the Bounty' followed with Marlon Brando, who was then in the

Cattleya maxima or Peek-a-boo Orchid was highly desired in the nineteenth >
century for its large flowers that have a smell similar to that of sweet peas.

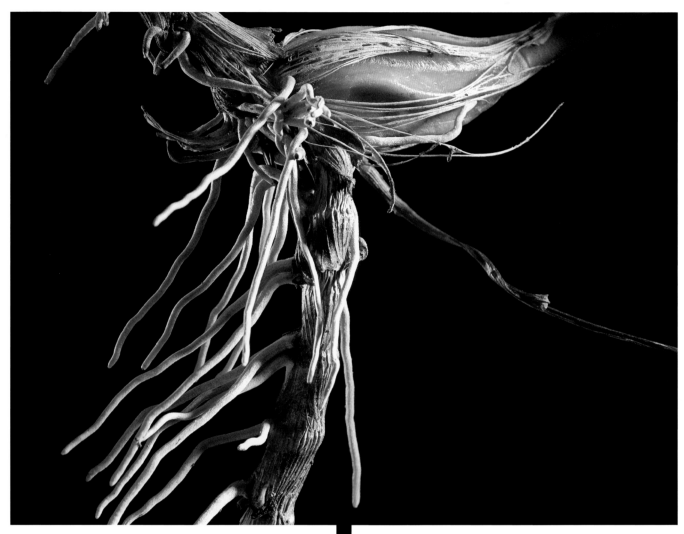

Pseudobulbs are thickened stems that retain food and water vital for the plant's survival.

early stages of his career. The most recent version was released in 1984, with Mel Gibson and Anthony Hopkins playing the leading roles.

Cattleyas — orchids with large and usually sweet smelling flowers — were responsible for the generation of much interest in orchids, becoming known in Europe under remarkable circumstances. About forty-five species of Cattleya are now known to grow in the wild in Central and South America. Early in the nineteenth century, William Cattley, a plant collector from London, noticed that a new arrival of ferns and mosses had been packed in the stiff, leathery leaves of plants that were unknown to him. Out of curiosity, he put the unknown plants in pots and in 1818 the first produced beautiful flowers, much to his surprise. This orchid was named *Cattleya labiata* after him. The original plants had been collected by a certain Mr. Swainson, but he had not informed anyone about their place of origin and subsequently he disappeared for some years in the jungle of New Zealand. All that was known was that the plants came from Brazil. All the large orchid growers sent plant hunters to that country between

1830 and 1880 to try to locate this *Cattleya* species. Searches in the area of Rio de Janeiro proved fruitless and it was not until 1889 that more were found again in the north of Brazil.

Since that time, many other species of Cattleya have been found. Their spectacular flowers have certainly contributed to the orchid craze which was to reach its peak during the nineteenth century. Cattleyas became particularly popular during the twentieth century because aristocratic ladies attached these ostentatious flowers to their dresses at dances and weddings. This is a tradition still alive among girls of the American upper classes when they attend their first dance. Regrettably, some species, such as *C. trianae* and *C. bowringiana*, have become very rare in nature due to over collection.

Orchid mania

A species which further promoted enthusiasm for orchids was the Butterfly Orchid, *Psychopsis papilio*, originating from Venezuela. The bizarre yellow and brown flowers

< This small **Macroclinium manabinum** originates from the Ecuadorian province of Manabi.

resemble a butterfly, with two dark shiny pellets at the base which seem to be eyes. The flowers are ten centimetres long and appear one after another on a flowering stem that can grow up to one metre in length. A single stem can produce flowers for years at regular intervals. It was this species responsible for the passion that William George Spencer Cavendish, the sixth Duke of Devonshire, developed for orchids. The Duke was fanatical about plants and had beautiful gardens planted at his Chatsworth estate. It was during exhibitions of the Royal Horticultural Society in 1833 that he came into contact with orchids and the spark was ignited in his heart at once. As a man of great means, he spent fortunes on building up an incredibly large and beautiful collection, which became the biggest and most famous of his time. This bachelor devoted the rest of his life to his orchid passion. He had a huge greenhouse built (90 metres long, 45 metres wide and 18 metres high) which could compete with the great greenhouses in the botanical gardens of the period. Since he was of the opinion that tropical orchids were not put up for sale enough in Europe, or, at least, not the most interesting ones, he organised private expeditions to collect them. He repeatedly sent his gardener John Gibson to the mountains of Assam, in the north of India, to bring back many known and unknown species. A considerable number of species were named after the Duke, such as *Cymbidium devonianum, Dendrobium devonianum, Oncidium cavendishianum,* and *Galeandra devoniana.*

The Duke of Devonshire's passion led to orchids becoming a status symbol in Britain. It became 'fashionable' for the Victorian aristocracy to possess an orchid collection, preferably with a large number of plants and some rare species. After a Butterfly Orchid (once again the same species) was exhibited in London in 1836 at a show of the Royal Horticultural Society, orchids became a national obsession. Queen Victoria became an ardent admirer. In her honour, a newly discovered species with graceful blue flowers was called *Dendrobium victoria reginae* and a Lady's Slipper Orchid was also given her name. For her Golden Jubilee in 1887, the English nurseryman Sander gave her a bouquet of orchids at least two metres high and a metre and a half wide. This masterpiece consisted of a bouquet of splendid flowers from dozens of different species, topped by a crown made from the golden blooms of Dendrobiums and Oncidiums, and the side displayed the letters V.R.I. in scarlet Epidendrums, the abbreviation for 'Victoria Regina et Imperatrix'.

Myriads of orchids

At the start of the nineteenth century, it was still believed that the orchid family had only a few representatives. Nowadays, we know better: orchids make up the second largest family of plants in the world (after the Composite family or the Asteraceae family). Orchids are found as far north as Alaska and the north of Sweden, and as far South as Vuurland, in any place on earth where there is plant life, from the polar circle to the equator. You can find them growing at sea level or in high altitudes such as the Himalayas and the Andes. They thrive equally well in damp regions such as tropical rain and cloud forests, as in open, dry areas of vegetation, such as the 'caatinga' in Brazil. In fact, many orchids are classed as 'xerophytes'. These are plants that are adapted to aridity; even numerous epiphytic species from damp regions are subjected to periodic dehydration. One of their adaptations is the formation of pseudobulbs, thickened stems in which the plant can store reserves of food and water.

The orchid family is not only special because of the large number of different species, but also because of the great variety between those species. No other family of plants contains such a diversity of colour, smell, shape, and size. The smallest orchids include *Bulbophyllum minutissimum*, whose pseudobulbs are as small as a pinhead, and *Bulbophyllum pygmaeum*, whose pseudobulbs look like minuscule scales. Another species vying for the title of smallest orchid is *Platystele jungermannoides*, a species from Central America with leaves from one to two millimetres long and flowers with a diameter of one millimetre. Meanwhile, the largest orchids grow up to five metres high — these include *Grammatophyllum speciosum* and *G. papuanum* from Southeast Asia.

Gradually, more and more people came to realise the incredible diversity to be found within the orchid family. In the course of the nineteenth century, more and more new species were brought back from the tropics. Whilst in 1823 only 134 species of orchids were known , this figure had risen to 6,000 by 1852. Three hundred new species of orchids were brought to England in the year 1837 alone. One species which caused a furore when it was imported into Europe was the *Odontoglossum crispum*. This species has a flower stalk up to one metre high with large, magnificent white flowers with a white and yellow lip adorned with red spots. Other forms have light pink or light yellow flowers, again some of them with red spots. The most beautiful examples of this species were sold in 1889 for more than 150 guineas per plant, an

The bizarre yellow and brown flowers of the Butterfly Orchid >
(Psychopsis papilio), so named due to its resemblance to that insect.

amount which represented a small fortune since it was considerably more than the average yearly salary at that time (the guinea is an old English currency worth 21 shillings). This orchid was discovered in 1841 in cloud forest in Colombia at a height of over two thousand metres. After its discovery, every mountain peak near Bogota was examined thoroughly as people searched for the plants that were in huge demand. Every plant encountered was plucked from its tree and entire woods were cut down so that the plants could be collected more easily. There were shipments of forty thousand plants per boat, but, sadly, only a small percentage survived the journey. Nowadays, there are hardly any remaining forests on the mountains near Bogota, and there are barely any plants of this orchid in the few parts which remain.

In the second half of the nineteenth century, the passion for orchids got out of hand. The orchid became a real object of worship. After the famous tulip mania, it was now the turn of orchids, but this craze was to last much longer. Since there was such a huge demand for orchids, their prices increased sharply. Growing orchids was the preserve of a few privileged and wealthy collectors, such as princes, dukes, and bankers. By the start of the twentieth century, there was talk of a real orchid mania. Henry Correvon (Album of Orchids of Europe, 1923, Geneva) explained: "Exotic orchids have played an important part in society during this century; like tulips in the past, they are almost being quoted on the stock exchange." Indeed, orchids became very expensive and sometimes fetched ridiculously high prices. In 1837, the Duke of Devonshire paid the sum of 120 guineas for a *Phalaenopsis amabilis*. Subsequently, the prices continued to rise for new or rare species. In 1881, 200 guineas were paid for a *Vanda sanderiana* which had been imported from the Philippines, whilst an *Aerides lawrenceae* fetched a sum of 6,150 francs. Around 1895, a plant of the madouxianum variety of *Odontoglossum crispum* was sold to a Quaker from Brussels for 35,000 Belgian francs. Record prices were fetched by *Odontoglossum crispum* plants, which sold for 1500 guineas per plant just before the First World War!

24

The magnificent **Odontoglossum splendidum** is a hybrid from a cross >
between **Odontoglossum crispum** and **O. ardentissimum.** The latter is
itself a hybrid between **O. crispum** and **O. nobile**.

Orchid hunter:
a dangerous profession

In England, the nurseries of James Veitch & Sons in Exeter and Chelsea were among the largest of the nineteenth century. They were renowned orchid growers and were also the first ones to make orchid hybrids. This firm employed no fewer than 23 professional orchid hunters, who were sent repeatedly to the tropics of American and Asia on expeditions between 1840 and 1912. Indeed, to satisfy the ever-growing demand, orchid hunters had to be sent to exotic places to fetch some plants, preferably rare or unknown species with spectacular blooms.

Another renowned grower was Frederick Sander, after whom two hundred orchids are named, mostly species with beautiful flowers. Sander was born in Bremen (Prussia) in 1847, but when he was eighteen he set off for London to look for work as a nurseryman. There he encountered orchids for the first time and became infatuated with them at once, a passion which he retained for the rest of his life. Within ten years, this energetic but demanding man owned his own business, which he continued to expand and geared it completely towards orchids. He devoted his entire life to the growth, import, and sale of these plants and obtained worldwide renown as 'the King of the Orchids'. He was appointed Royal Orchid Grower by Queen Victoria, and the Romanoffs, the Russian Royal Family, appointed him as Baron of the Holy Russian Empire. Most European royal families purchased orchids from him and he was, for example, the only supplier to the Baron of Rothschild, a wealthy banker who lived in the sumptuous castle of Waddesdon Manor in England. He was also supplier to the Duke of Devonshire, of course.

Sander managed an orchid nursery in St Albans, thirty kilometres north of London, and later opened a second nursery, this time in mainland Europe near Bruges, Belgium. At St Albans, there were dozens of greenhouses, some of them sixty metres long. These greenhouses accommodated thousands of growing *Odontoglossum crispum* plants which were worth a fortune in those days. There was also a 100 metre long display greenhouse which housed giant plants. These included nine giant specimens of *Cymbidium lowianum*, which displayed a hundred and fifty flower stalks when they flowered!

To continue to sell the most beautiful and most exclusive orchids, Sander had at his disposal a good team of almost forty orchid hunters who scoured every jungle in search of new and sensational species. Orchid hunting was an extremely dangerous and demanding profession. These men were given the assignment of searching for plants in remote and unexplored places where they faced all sorts of dangers. They were alone save for the company of their guides and bearers for months and sometimes years. Many died during these expeditions. They often found their way into the territory of tribes who objected to their presence, and many of them were shot or fell victim to head-hunters. Equally treacherous were the wild animals, mosquitoes and snakes, as well as deadly diseases and infections. Many died of fever and exhaustion. Others went missing and disappeared without trace. Their work was difficult and demanding, because even when they had found the required plants, it usually required daring exploits to get the collected spoils back to a boat sailing for Europe. There were hardly any passable roads from the jungle to the port and the means of transport were often defective.

Masdevallia ignea is found in Peru in areas over three thousand metres high. >

Oncidium phalaenopsis comes from Ecuador where it flourishes
in cool conditions at an altitude of 2700 to 2900 meters.

Hunters not only had to keep an eye open for the numerous dangers of the jungle, but they also had to be aware of the tricks of rival collectors. William Arnold, a young German, was sent by Sander to Venezuela on his first trip to look for *Masdevallia tovarensis* plants. His journey started badly. He was questioned by station officials in Waterloo Station in London about the moss which he had taken with him to pack the orchids. This problem was solved, but due to this exchange his fellow travellers knew that Arnold was travelling to Caracas. One of the men in his train compartment introduced himself as a sales representative who knew nothing about orchids and said that he, too, was travelling to Venezuela. In fact, his name was White, an orchid hunter employed by Low, a rival company. Mr White asked a number of seemingly innocent questions in an attempt to obtain information about his naïve rival's mission. In the course of their journey, Sander informed Arnold by post of his travelling companion's real identity and this revelation almost led to a duel even before they had reached their destination. This was Arnold's introduction to the treacherous world of orchid hunting. Part of the work consisted of following other plant hunters to find out where they had found orchids. There were some dirty tricks played, and this was all part of the wars which growers waged against each other to be the first to launch new species on the market and offer the largest number of special plants for sale. Na-

back in a shipment of *Paphiopedilum insigne*, a more general species which grows in numerous places in the Himalayas. All the major orchid companies sent expeditions to the north of India in the hope of finding such plants. Sander entertained similar hopes, too, but first of all he contacted the lady in question in the hope of finding out some more information. During their discussion about orchids, he raised the subject of the Far East and asked her frankly if she happened to have any relatives or acquaintances there, and indeed she did. Her son owned a large tea plantation on the border of Bhutan, north of Assam. On request, he was even given the address of the plantation and he duly sent the plant hunter Forsterman there at once. Forsterman was forbidden to say anything about orchids, so he acted as if he were looking for work to gain experience of tea plantations. There was no work available, but he was invited by the manager to stay there as a guest. During his stay, he was unable to detect any *Paphiopedilum spicerianum*. However, the manager told him of a trip to Bhutan, during which he had found an orchid which caused a great sensation in London. It had been a terrible journey because the Bhutanese were hostile and the jungle was swarming with tigers. Forsterman left the plantation the next day and set off in search of these orchids. He journeyed through steep and rocky areas, wading upstream in the ice-cold water of every river he came to. After an exhausting two-day trek, he stumbled across a large patch of orchids at the top of a cliff face just before sunset. He made a bamboo ladder and climbed the rocks. This was the plant which he was looking for, and it was growing there in large quantities! It didn't take long to gather the plants, but the return journey proved to be long and dangerous. He had to kill a tiger which was threatening a Bhutanese village before the village residents would agree to work for him as carriers. Eventually, he managed to bring thousands of live plants back to England so that on 9th March 1884, Sander was able to offer forty thousand plants for sale at auction.

tives were also bribed in attempts to find out where rivals were heading, while growers paid spies (employees of rival companies) for information about their competitors.

Good secret services are crucially important in any war. Sander was unrivalled in his drive to find out all the required information, as is apparent from the story of the discovery of *Paphiopedilum spicerianum*. In 1878, an English lady had a special flowering *Paphiopedilum* (Lady's Slipper) in her collection, which she sold to the company Veitch. Each offshoot of this plant was sold for more than its weight in gold. When enquiries were made about the origin of the plant, the lady merely said that the plant had been brought

In 1890, Sander sent another orchid hunter Micholitz on an expedition to New Guinea in search of a special species of *Dendrobium phalaenopsis*. This variety had been given as a gift by the Englishman Forbes to the Royal Botanic Gardens at Kew in 1857. After studying the account of the journey written by Forbes, he concluded that he must have found the plants on the remote and dangerous island of New Guinea. Micholitz reached the port of Larat on this island and was fortunate enough to be able to travel a few days later with a group of tribal chiefs who were going to a meet-

Vanda Gordon Dillon 'Lea' is derived from **Vanda sanderiana**;
it is a hybrid of **V.** *'Madame Rattana'* x **V.** *'Bangkok Blue'*.

ing in a nearby cove. He attended a long and tiring ceremony during which painted warriors with spears and clubs danced for hours on end and brought gruesome offers. In order to have some peace and quiet, he fled to a nearby forest where he found the plants which he was looking for. He had a few thousand plants put on a ship, but a fire broke out at night whilst he was sleeping in a port on the quayside. The entire shipment of orchids was ruined! Micholitz sent a report to Sander to ask what he should do next, and the answer was that he should return to look for a new shipment. Micholitz responded that it was too late because of the rainy season. Sander's reply to this was abrupt: "Go back!" And so, Micholitz went back, but his arrival on the island was delayed by several months. He had to find a new patch where orchids were growing because he had completely ravaged the first. After

numerous searches, he eventually found an even larger site. However, these plants were growing on limestone cliffs amidst human skulls and bones! This was the burial place of a tribe where the dead had been laid. Initially, the natives refused to fetch the orchids because they did not want to disturb the spirits of their ancestors. Tempted by the offer of numerous gifts, they eventually agreed to dig up as many plants as they could. When these orchids were put up for sale at auction in London, they caused a sensation, especially a plant displayed growing out of a human skull. Two years later, Sander's head gardener asked Micholitz to go and fetch more plants from the same location, but he replied that he would rather preserve his own skull. This was a wise decision because later in that same year the orchid collector White was killed and eaten by the Papuans in New Guinea.

The discovery of **Euanthe (Vanda) sanderiana** is an exciting story.

One of Sander's most successful plant hunters was Carl Roebelin, who discovered the sensational *Vanda sanderiana*. In 1879, he was assigned to explore the island of Mindanao in the Philippines in search of new species. This island was extremely remote and impenetrable and inhabited by cannibals and tribes which waged war against each other constantly. Roebelin had heard from some natives that there was supposed to be a red orchid in the north of the island. According to the descriptions, this sounded like a *Phalaenopsis*. A red variety of *Phalaenopsis* was unknown in those days and Roebelin commenced the journey (1000 kilometres) in a small boat full of natives. However, when he eventually arrived, he did not find what he was looking for, despite various attempts. However, he talked to the native inhabitants and heard stories about a

blue orchid with flowers as big as a plate. This storybook flower was supposed to grow near Lake Magindanao in the centre of the island.

Roebelin changed his plans and decided to go there. He was fortunate enough to be able to travel together with a Chinese man who was going to recover his debts from the local tribe. They travelled up a river and came to a huge lake. As they approached their destination, however, a storm caused their boat to sink. All were able to survive and were welcomed by the local tribe. However, when the Chinese man went to demand payment from his debtors, a dispute erupted. Just as the dispute was threatening to run out of control, a neighbouring hostile tribe attacked their hosts. The tribe which had welcomed them as guests were able to defeat their enemies and everyone laid down to rest in the evening. Roebelin spent the night in a tree hut, but in the middle of the night he was woken up by a terrible noise and movements all around him. He was rattled and shaken inside the tree hut, and this continued for some time. Around him he heard the cries of people who had fallen out of their huts and were thrown to their death. It was an earthquake!

The tree hut was largely destroyed, but Roebelin survived. Furthermore, through the broken floor of the tree hut, he saw some absolutely beautiful orchids beneath him, the plants which he had been looking for. He collected the plants and returned to the port along the coast, but the entire town was destroyed. In fact, Roebelin had experienced the worst ever earthquake in the Philippines. There was nothing he could do except dry out a few plants for herbarium samples as evidence of his incredible find. He sent the rest of the plants back to Europe as soon as the next boat arrived. However, the long delay meant all the plants died before they reached their destination.

Roebelin also made drawings of the flowers, but when these were seen in England, he was regarded as a fake because no one believed that such flowers could exist. Sander sent the dried plants to the botanist Reichenbach, who described these new *Vanda* and named them in honour of Frederick Sander. This was only a partial victory. The first living plants of this kind that eventually reached England were not collected by Roebelin, but by his arch-rival Boxall, who worked for Low, Sander's fiercest competitor.

The orchid hunters from the nineteenth century had no ecological conscience. They scoured the world for unique and rare species that could be sold as expensively as possible. If there were a surplus of plants at a habitat, the remaining plants were destroyed so that no one else would be able to collect them. In this way, they hoped to secure exclusivity. Furthermore, entire trees sometimes had to be felled in order to collect plants that grew too high. In order to get the magnificent *Odontoglossum crispum* in Columbia, a plant hunter collected about ten thousand plants in one visit, but had to cut down at least 4000 trees in the process! The director of the botanic garden in Zurich at that time wrote that "orchid hunters are not satisfied with the collection of three to five hundred specimens of every beautiful

Vanda tricolor is a species from Indonesia with attractively patterned flowers and a wonderful scent.

species, but they have to skim the whole land and don't leave anything around for miles. The surroundings of Quito and Cuenca are completely ravaged and not a single *Odontoglossum* can be found. These modern plant hunters spare nothing or no one. This is no longer plant collection, but pure robbery and I ask myself why public opinion does not protest against it."

Towards the end of the nineteenth century, the number of orchid hunters working for Sander was greatly reduced: one was killed in Mexico, another shot in Brazil, a third disappeared for good on a trip along the Orinoco, a fourth

died in Panama, yet another was murdered in Ecuador, a sixth in Madagascar, and a seventh in the Far East. Another plant hunter disappeared in Madagascar, but was found again a few years later by another plant hunter. He lived in a settlement where he had married the chief's daughter. His explanation was: "I had to get married or otherwise they would have eaten me!" A few years later, this unfortunate man succeeded in escaping. Sander's surviving orchid hunters handed in their resignations. Everyone who worked for him complained about the lack of financial rewards until they successfully completed their mission abroad. Eventually, in the nineties, of the forty orchid hunters that had worked for Sander, but two men

remained, Forget and Micholitz. Both of them were to work for Sander until 1914, when the demand for orchids dropped to almost zero because of the war and the resulting collapsed economy. In any case searching for orchids had also become increasingly more difficult because of the scarcity of plants in their natural surroundings. Micholitz wrote in 1913: "You must not forget that the plants are getting scarcer every year…"

Aquarelles were an important marketing tool for selling orchids: **Odontoglossum crispum var. Bousiesianum** by Albert Goossens for the series Dictionnaire Iconographique des Orchidées.

Bitter competition and rivalry

At the beginning of the nineteenth century, England was the centre of tropical orchid cultivation, but Belgium was also developing into an important venue for their study and cultivation. This was largely due to the work of Jean Linden, who is known as 'the Father of Orchids'. As a young person starting work in 1835, he made several expeditions for the Belgian government, first for two years to Brazil, and then to Venezuela, the Antilles, and Cuba. After this, he started a horticultural company which was initially established in Luxemburg, but moved to Brussels a short time later. He also sent a number of orchid hunters to Latin America and Congo. In total, Linden imported no less than eighteen hundred orchid species! Several bear his name, such as *Cattleyopsis lindenii* and *Phragmipedium lindenii*. The increasing importance of Belgium as a centre for orchid cultivation is illustrated by the fact that Sander 'the Orchid King' and one of the largest English orchid growers, moved a part of his company to Bruges. In fact, Linden became Sander's chief rival and in 1860 he was perhaps the largest supplier of orchids in Europe. There was a ruthless fight between their plant hunters. For example, the Belgian Claes sent the local police in Brazil after his French rival Forget (who worked for Sander). They confiscated his plants on the basis of some local law or other, while in the meantime Claes had already been able to send a shipment of orchids to Europe. Sander also tried to get the extremely successful

Bungeroth, one of Linden's employees, to work for him. However, he refused and blamed Sander for starting the bitter rivalry between the companies. Because of the large quantities of orchids pouring into Europe in the meantime, plant prices started to fall. In 1894, Sander decided to build a second orchid nursery around Bruges, which had to be bigger than the one in St Albans. He bought a piece of land and built one greenhouse after another. There were 240 in all! In addition to orchids other plants were grown in huge quantities, including a quarter of a million laurel trees. This company was the largest horticultural enterprise in the world at the time. From this establishment Sander sold large quantities of orchids to European nobles and bankers, and even to the Pope.

Both Linden and Sander published several illustrated books of orchids. Since there were no coloured photographs, these drawings showed orchid lovers what the flowers of (newly discovered) species looked like enticing amateurs to buy these beautiful flowers. As a result, watercolours of orchids became an important instrument for marketing orchids. Linden published "Lindenia. Iconographie des orchidées" and "Pescatorea. Iconographie des orchidées". Both works have been republished recently — Lindenia is a deluxe edition with splendid layouts of orchid illustrations.

Sander was the editor of the Reichenbachiana, a luxurious series of orchid drawings. It consisted of four volumes dedicated to the Queen of England, the Empress of Germany, the Empress of Russia, and the Queen of Belgium respectively. Each volume of the imperial edition weighed 22kg and measured 74cm by 60cm. All the drawings, most of which were by H.G. Moon, were printed as a chromolithography with twenty different kinds of ink. It is little wonder that this monumental edition almost brought Sander to ruin!

The Reichenbachiana series was named after Professor Heinrich Gottlieb Reichenbach, a German botanist who, after the death of Linden, became the orchid expert of Europe. It was Reichenbach who described the innovations that Sander sent him, and their collaboration lasted a few decades. They both had an almost freakish devotion to orchids, and Reichenbach had one of the largest herbarium of that time. When Reichenbach died at the age of 56, the scientific world was shocked by the announcement of his will. He had left his collections to a museum in Vienna, provided that the dried specimens and the orchid drawings

Jean Linden gave his name to the variety **Odontoglossum crispum var. lindenii**.

would not be displayed until 25 years after his death. This was a sad blow for botanists because Reichenbach's herbarium was a reference collection which they wanted to consult to make comparisons with newly collected plants (photographs of herbaria were of course not yet available).

A number of watercolour artists became famous as a result of their orchid illustrations. Albert Goossens was a talented Belgian painter who produced hundreds of such watercolours. These were collated for the 'Dictionnaire iconographique des orchidées'. Goossens was made honorary member of the American Orchid Society (AOS) because of the support he had given to orchid science. Most of his watercolours were bought by the AOS and are still displayed at the seat of this association in Boston. Artists such as Goossens made it a matter of honour to represent the plants accurately. Other painters did not always depict them precisely and were put under pressure by their customers to make the flowers prettier than they actually were. This even went so far that a customer instituted legal proceedings against a grower because the purchased flowers did not correspond to the represented images.

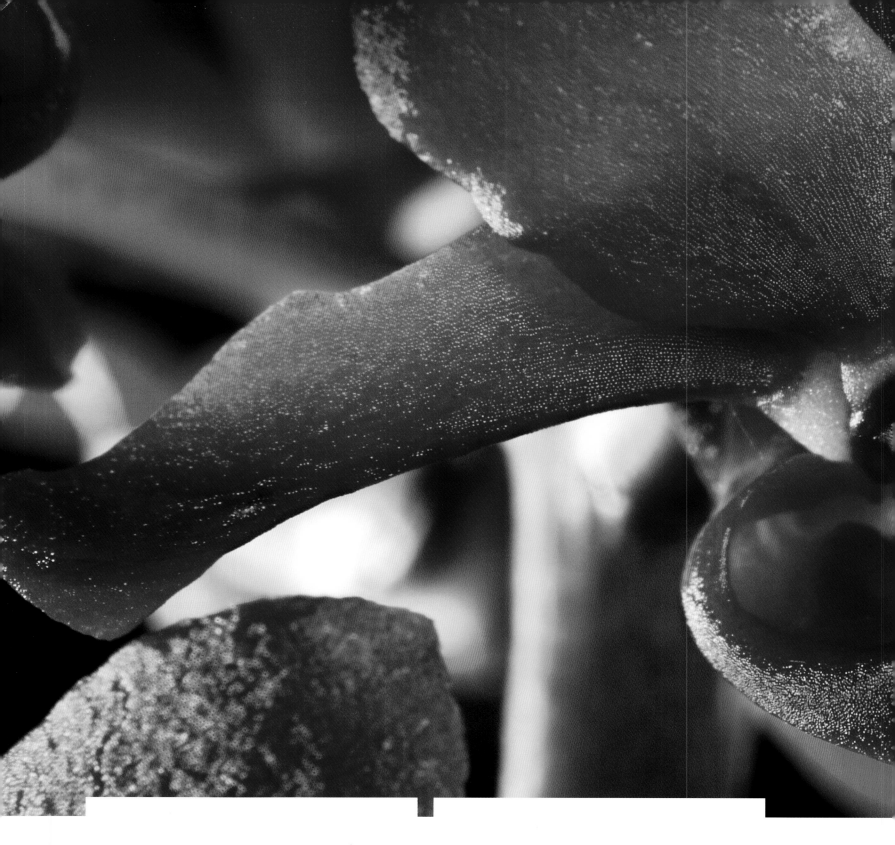

Parasites?
No, epiphytes!

Rhynchostylis gigantea var. rubra

Although there were many tropical orchids shipped to Europe in the nineteenth century, most plants perished initially because of poor growing methods. This was the consequence of a big misunderstanding. It was known that these plants grew on trees like mistletoe. Therefore people thought orchids were parasites, which draw the sap from its host tree. One could read in the English magazine Botanical Register in 1815 that "the cultivation of these tropical parasitic plants had been considered impossible for a long time. It would also therefore be no use trying to cultivate suitable trees for each kind in greenhouses."

Nevertheless, people found the flower so magnificent that many plant lovers continued to try to grow the tropical orchids, almost always with fatal results for the plants. Eventually, however, it became clear that tree-growing orchids were not parasites but epiphytes, plants that simply use trees as support. They do not damage the trees, but live from the moisture and humus present on the branches. Seventy percent of all orchid species live epiphytically, especially tropical orchids, whereas most orchids in temperate regions are rooted in the ground (terrestrial species). Some orchids, however, have no chlorophyll, and these are saprophytes, living off dead and decaying organic material. This is the case for the Bird Nest Orchid (*Neottia nidus-avis*), a species found in the temperate forests of Europe and Asia.

The epiphytic lifestyle of most orchids constitutes a clever strategy in the tropical rainforest where fights rage for every square centimetre of soil. This competition is inevitably won by trees because their roots can grow deep in the ground and they can form a large canopy. These forest giants therefore not only occupy the ground but also intercept most of the light so that under their canopy it is quite dark. Light definitely means life for plants. As a solution to this problem, orchids grow on tree branches high in the canopy where there is sufficient light. This means, however, that they have to be economical with water and food because these resources are more limited high up in the trees. The water which they get comes from the rain and also from dew or mist in some areas, while they get their food from dead leaves and other matter or soil that is blown by the wind. This is why orchids are not the fastest growing plants by a long way, and they often have to ration themselves carefully with the little that they manage to secure. The epiphytic growth habit of orchids also means that their roots are very aerated. This is important when making a choice regarding a container mixture to cultivate orchids: if the soil mixture does not let sufficient air through, the roots will start rotting fast. Orchids like plenty of ventilation, which is why there are often ventilators present in specialist glasshouses to mimic natural air circulation.

The fact that orchids are not parasites, but epiphytes, became clear only gradually. It took some time to find out the right method to cultivate them. It was thought, for example, that orchids liked a smothering hot and scalding humid environment, whereas they actually needed plenty of ventilation or even drafts. At the end of the eighteenth century, orchids were even put in a stovehouse, in a smothering atmosphere where the poor plants could not survive for long. Moreover, there are many orchids that like a temperate cool environment, especially orchids originating from cloud forests such as those in the Andes. Finally, many orchids need a rest period in which they are given little water and often low temperatures; otherwise they will not come into bloom. Due to an increase in knowledge about the environmental factors in their natural habitats, more and more people have succeeded in getting orchids to

flower or, even better, to have them survive and flower again many times. It took a lot of time for this knowledge to emerge, and in the meantime tens of thousands of orchids succumbed, perishing either during the boat trip or during their cultivation in Europe. In 1819, a nurseryman wrote that only a few plants had survived from an import of thousands. Before the plants ended up in cultivation, they had passed through a real war of attrition. They were taken out of the trees in far away countries and brought to a port where they were shipped to England or another European country. The boat trip was very long and the travelling conditions were anything but ideal for the plants. And so, it is understandable that a botanist stated that England was the graveyard of tropical orchids for half a century.

Rhynchostylis gigantea var. rubra is an epiphytic orchid with thick, > fleshy aerial roots for the absorption of water.

Vanilla

Vanilla humblotii grows on the Comoro Islands.

One of the first tropical orchids imported to Europe was vanilla. It is also the orchid with the greatest economic interest worldwide, being the only one sold on a large scale for non-ornamental purposes.

The vanilla is a 'liana' which climbs into trees and can grow up to 30 metres long. About a hundred species belong to the genus *Vanilla*, which grow in the tropics worldwide. However, only species native to Central and South America possess perfumed seed pods. Most of the *Vanilla* species have greenish or white flowers. The species bred for commercial trade are *Vanilla planifolia, V. pompona* and *V. tahitensis*. It is the seed pods of these species which disperse the strong vanilla aroma. The name vanilla originates from the Spanish word 'vainilla' ('vaina' for short), which means sheath or envelope, the word also used for the beans of legumes. The seed pods of vanilla are narrow and elongated and reminiscent of beans. To develop their special aroma, vanilla beans have to be dried and fermented. This process is very important for the development of a fine aroma, and all together takes about eight months.

However, there are also vanilla species of which the beans and the flowers smell strongly without being dried. This is the case of *Vanilla aromatica*, a species which originates from the Amazon area and is cultivated in gardens in Brazil for the beauty and exquisite scent of the flowers. This species contains one percent vanillin in its seed pods. Another species with scented pods is *Vanilla palmarum*, which has orange yellow flowers and is used to spice food; it is also used as an aphrodisiac. This species grows high on palm trees from Bolivia to Brazil.

The Spanish discovered vanilla orchids (*Vanilla planifolia*) during their conquest expeditions in Mexico. There they were cultivated by the Aztecs, who called them 'tlilxochitl' (black flower). The flowers are not actually black, but the vanilla beans are once they are treated. The Aztecs mixed vanilla with crushed cacao beans ('cacaoatl') to make a chocolate drink, to which corn was also added. No sugar was mixed in it, instead it was spiced up with hot peppers and pimento.

Vanilla was brought to Europe for the first time in 1510. Seventy years later, a cocoa drink with vanilla was presented to the King and Queen of Spain, and after that this beverage quickly became popular at the court of Madrid and with all the Spanish nobility. From there this pleasure spread gradually all over Europe during the course of the seventeenth century. Louis XIV, the French Sun King, and his queen drank hot chocolate with vanilla in the morning on an empty stomach and Madame de Pompadour was also keen on it.

Initially, vanilla was sourced from the forests of Mexico, but soon the plants were cultivated in other parts of Central and South America. It was only during the course of the eighteenth century, with the building of greenhouses, that it became possible to cultivate vanilla plants in Europe.

From the end of the eighteenth century onwards, vanilla was introduced in colonies or overseas territories of France: in La Réunion (then called Bourbon), Mauritius, Tahiti and Madagascar, and in the nineteenth century by the Spanish in the Philippines and the Dutch in Java. Although the plants could be cultivated, there was no natural pollinator, so they never produced pods.

The story goes that the discovery of the pollination of vanilla was made at the beginning of the nineteenth century by a French landowner on the island of Bourbon (La Réunion), or actually by his slave Edmond. This landowner had received cuttings of a vanilla plant and managed to cultivate a plant that had climbed into an old mango tree. The orchid produced sweet-scented flowers, but seed pods were never formed. A young slave of the plantation owner used to climb into this tree whenever he was frustrated or angry. In his rage against his master, who was very concerned for his vanilla plant, he folded up the vanilla flowers and in so doing pollinated the flowers without knowing it. His master noticed that fruits were forming, and he connected this to the presence of the black boy in the tree. He questioned him to find out what exactly he did to the flowers, and this boy showed him what he did. De facto, the male and female organs of the flowers are separated by a husk, which has to be broken through for pollination. This in effect is what happened when the flowers were folded. This observation formed the start of the vanilla cultivation on this island, which was economically successful and therefore soon expanded to the islands of Mauritius, Madagascar and the Comoros. Vanilla is still bred on La Réunion and 'Bourbon' vanilla is believed to have the best quality. Because the pollinators do not flourish there, the pollination is still carried out manually by women, who can pollinate up to 1800 flowers per day.

Although vanilla was mainly added to chocolate, it was also added to other beverages in the nineteenth century, such as coffee. Gradually vanilla was also used in all sorts of sweets and desserts, ice cream, and biscuits. However, vanilla is also delicious used in the preparations of fish and mussels, in rhubarb or with cherries. Tobacco was, and still is, perfumed with vanilla, giving it a sweet aroma.

A number of medicinal properties are imputed to vanilla. Badianus wrote in 1522 that vanilla was used as a herb, for the taste, or as a drink for general health. Various medicinal properties were imputed to it. In the 'Flore médicale des Antilles', Descourtilz (1829) states that vanilla possessed powerful sexually stimulating properties, as well as stomach healing, wind expulsion, and warming and menstruation inducing properties. This herb was also seen as effective against melancholia.

Vanilla is also used as raw material in perfumery, and the basis for numerous famous fragrances. The first synthetic perfume ever made, and which caused a revolution in the business, was Jicky. It was made in 1889 by André Guerlain and contains vanillin and coumarin. The more recent Shalimar of Guerlain also contains vanilla, to which it gives an exuberant, sensual note. The renowned Chanel N° 5, which was designed in 1921 by Ernest Beaux and which is still prestigious now, contains vanilla aroma. Another example is Opium, designed in 1976 by Yves Saint Laurent, which disperses a mysterious and eastern scent. The vanilla, which finds an application in the perfumery, pertains to the species *Vanilla pompona*.

With all these applications, vanilla is a crop with immense economic value. In the United States, 1262 tons were imported in 1992; consumption in European countries now amounts to between 0.13 and 4.6 grams of vanillin per inhabitant per year, depending upon the country. However, vanillin, the substance that gives vanilla its aroma, is increasingly being produced in an industrial manner. One of the raw materials used for this purpose is wood pulp, because its structure (lignin) is closely related to that of vanillin. Eugenol, a product from clove, cinnamon, or 'allspice' (*Pimenta dioica*) can also be used. However, synthetic vanilla never has the same delicate aroma as the natural vanilla.

Synthetic or natural vanilla can cause allergies in some people. This is called 'vanillism', and it can give rise to various symptoms ranging from headaches, dizziness, insomnia, skin eruption, infection of the retina, and infection of the eyelids. Labourers in biscuit factories have been known to develop eczema on their hands due to the handling of biscuits in which vanilla is present. There are also known cases of allergy after people have consumed ice cream with vanilla flavour.

Orchids with a
genealogy

After pollination, the next crucial step for bringing orchids into cultivation was the production of hybrids. The orchid family is an immensely large group. The calculations and estimates of the quantity of the species found in the wild oscillate usually between twenty and thirty thousand species. This means that the orchid family is the second largest on earth, after the *Compositae* or Asteraceae, which include daisies, chicory and thistles. This also means that approximately one in ten flowering species is an orchid. The exact number is not known because many species have not yet been discovered or described, and also because some species have been described repeatedly under the same name. However, apart from the wild species, there are also man-made hybrids — their quantity easily exceeds one hundred thousand. The number of hybrids therefore amounts to a multiple of the original number, and this will increase substantially for sure! This exceptionally large number of hybrids can be attributed to their ability to cross with species from other genera. In general, this is not possible within other plant families, unless recently developed special techniques are used. For example, potatoes and tomatoes cannot cross, although both belong to the nightshade family (Solanaceae), because they belong to two different genera. With orchids however, this is possible. Moreover, the resulting hybrids can again be crossed mutually, or be crossed again with other species so that an almost unlimited combination of hybrids can be made.

The Chinese hybrid **Brassolaeliocattleya** *Chia Lin 'China Tian'* has an impressive and complicated pedigree.

The first artificial hybrid was made in 1854 by John Dominy, who was the head gardener of the renowned English nursery James Veitch & Sons. He crossed *Calanthe furcata* with *Calanthe masuca*; the resulting plant was named *Calanthe x Dominyi*. This was therefore a cross within the same genus, and there followed several other hybrids between closely related species. The first cross between species of different genera was made in 1863, when *Cattleya mossiae* was combined with *Laelia crispa*. These so called inter-generic crosses were given new names; for example, Laeliocattleya was the name given to the combination of *Laelia* and *Cattleya*. In 1892, the first tri-generic cross was made, between the species *Sophronitis grandiflora* and the hybrid *Laeliocattleya x schilleriana*;

The parents of **Maclellanara** *'Pagan Love Song'* are **Odontocidium** >
'Tiger Butter' and **Brassia verrucosa.**

the resulting plant was called Sophrolaeliocattleya Veitchi-ana (SLC for short). In the same way Brassolaeliocattleya (BLC for short) was formed through a hybrid of *Brassavola* with *Laelia* and *Cattleya*. A recent example of this is Brassolaeliocattleya Chia Lin 'China Tian', a Chinese cross which was registered in 1989 and which possesses an impressive and complicated genealogy (see below). No less than eleven species of *Cattleya*, three species of *Laelia*, and one species of *Brassavola* were used to reach this combination, and that required sixty-two steps! The first of these steps goes back to 1856, when *Cattleya dowiana* was crossed with *Cattleya warscewiczii*. The end result is a plant with very large flowers with a special Bordeaux colour. The name of the hybrid is BLC Chia Lin, but since the plants which are obtained from crosses are variable, usually the name of a form or clone is added in quotation marks, 'China Tian' in this case. Therefore, there are other clones from this same hybrid which look slightly different, for example 'Shin Su', a clone with dark purple flowers.

Another example is Brassolaeliocattleya Ports of Paradise 'Green Ching Hwa'. This has similar large flowers, but they are completely yellow in colour. Note that the same species of *Brassavola* is always used for such hybrids, namely *Brassavola digbyana*.

While the possibilities for making hybrids are almost unlimited, with the option of four or more genera, the system for giving new names to these inter-generic crossings by joining together (parts of) the original names of the genus cannot be sustained. Therefore new names have been generated with names of researchers or orchid cultivators using the suffix '-ara'. One of the first of such names was *Vuylstekeara*, named after the Belgian grower Charles Vuylsteke, who made numerous marvellous hybrids early in the twentieth century. Vuylstekearas are crosses of *Cochlioda x Miltonia x Odontoglossum*. Another example is Maclellanara, a cross between *Odontoglossum, Oncidium* and *Brassia*.

Brassolaeliocattleya *Ports of Paradise 'Green Ching Hwa'* has large, yellow-green flowers.

< **Epicattleya** *Rene Marques 'Flame Thrower'* is a hybrid of
Epidendrum pseudepidendrum and **Cattleya Claesiana.**

From exclusive collector's item to everyday domestic plant

During the course of the nineteenth century and in the beginning of the twentieth century, orchids were exclusive plants belonging to rich collectors. With the coming of the two world wars and the economic depression of that time, the orchid mania collapsed. In 1917, for example, the colossal greenhouse of the Duke of Devonshire was blown up with dynamite, because its maintenance and heating had become too expensive.

After the Second World War, a completely new era dawned for orchid growers and amateurs. Orchids became cheaper and fell within the budget of the masses. One of the most important steps in this process was the invention of techniques to germinate orchids on a large scale. Although keeping orchids alive and even making the crosses during the second half of the nineteenth century was gradually refined little by little, people did not know how to germinate them. If the seeds were sown in earth, no plants grew, except when the seeds were strewn around the mother plant. By doing so they did germinate in some cases, and some young plants could be obtained, but the result was very inconsistent.

In the beginning of the twentieth century, the Frenchman Noël Bernard and the German Burgeff made the discovery that orchid seeds germinated in the vicinity of a Rhizoctonia-mould. This fungus was added to a sterilised fermentation substrate of peat on which the orchid seeds were sown, and resulted in a good germination. The technique made it possible to multiply orchids in large quantities, something that previously had not been possible. Now thousands of plants could be cultivated from one seed pod.

After Noël Bernard had communicated his findings in April 1908 at an international horticultural exhibition and congress in Ghent, sowing and hybridisation soon became a sport for orchid growers. Evidence of this is the creation of the *Cymbidium pauwelsii* cross in 1911. The orchid collector Pauwels possessed a specimen of *Cymbidium insigne*, while Count de Hemptinne had a plant of *Cymbidium lowianum* in his collection. Both gentlemen decided to cross these plants, dividing the seeds between them on the understanding that the first one to make a plant blossom from this could put his name to the resulting cross. And so, it became *Cymbidium pauwelsii*...

How the fungus promoted orchid germination was not completely clear. The explanation was discovered by Knudson who found that orchid seeds only germinate in nature after they have been penetrated by a fungus. This fungus passes sugars on to them, providing them with the necessary energy to germinate. Orchid seeds have insufficient food reserves of their own to do this. This is not surprising really, because their seeds are dust-fine; they weigh between 0.3 and 14 milligrams. They are too small to contain endosperm, the nutritive tissue present in the seeds of other plants. The advantage of their small scale is that they can be dispersed

Phalaenopsis are rewarding houseplants that can keep >
blooming almost throughout the year: this hybrid is *'Detroit'*.

Phalaenopsis javanica

The scented **Phalaenopsis mariae** originates from the Philippines.

by the wind, sometimes at a distance of dozens of kilometres. A single seed pod will usually contain thousands of seeds, or even more. The record of the largest quantity of seeds is probably held by the orchid *Cycnoches chlorochilon*, which can produce up to 3.7 million seeds per seed pod.

Charles Darwin calculated that if all the seeds from a single pod germinated, the whole Isle of Wight (the largest of England's islands, with a surface area of 380 square kilometres) would be covered in orchids. If then each orchid in its turn formed seeds, and if all these were to germinate, the whole earth would be covered with orchids. In truth, though, only a miniscule number of the seeds would be able to germinate. This is because the seeds usually do not end up in favourable conditions, namely near the right fungus and the right quantities of moisture and light. Research into the South African species *Aerangis verdickii* has shown that, on average, only one in a million seeds germinate in nature.

Knudson's discovery also allowed him to develop a more efficient sowing technique, the asymbiotic method. He developed a fully synthetic growing medium with sugars, mineral salts, vitamins and other necessary growth

substances. From then on, orchids were sown in growing tubes on this complex growing medium. This method speeded up their cultivation significantly, but most still needed four to seven years to become flowering plants from seed. However, valuable hybrids from seed cannot be propagated, because the resulting plants are different from the parent plant. This shortcoming was remedied by the development of methods to clone plants, i.e. to make exact copies of them. It started in around 1960 with the *in vitro* propagation (also called micro-propagation) of Cymbidiums, developed by the Frenchman Morel. It thus became possible to cultivate thousands of plants in glass vials or test tubes from one immature bud. In several European countries, and primarily the Netherlands, an entire industry of large nurseries developed, which flooded the European market with *Cymbidium* hybrids from the nineteen seventies onwards. Varieties with white, yellow, red, brown, orange, and even green flowers were created. The large waxy blooms of these Cymbidiums contrast greatly with the varieties cultivated for centuries in China and Japan.

Thanks to the development of efficient sowing techniques and micro-propagation, the trade in orchids became an industry which now generates several millions of euros annually worldwide. In Europe, the Netherlands is the trendsetter: at the Aalsmeer flower auction, twenty million orchids (in pots) are traded each year, and this quantity keeps increasing. The worldwide retail trade of orchids has an estimated turnover of approximately nine billion dollars.

Since the eighties, *Phalaenopsis* plants have been offered for sale as flowering plants. They are very graceful houseplants, which can bloom almost the whole year: the individual flowers last for several months, and when a flower stalk has ceased blossoming, it can shoot again at the base, where another stalk can develop. The plants do require a lot of warmth (preferably above 15°C), a fair quantity of light, but no direct sun, weekly watering and, once in a while, some nutrients in the water. They will then reward the proud owner with an abundance of beautiful flowers.

In the past, only white and pink crosses were sold, but nowadays a whole range of yellow, red and purple varieties are available. Hybrids are made with other genera, so that apricot and salmon pink flowers are produced. In Taiwan forms were cultivated with petals which are arc shaped (peloric forms), and also *Phalaenopsis* of the Harlequin type. These are crosses with large dark purple stains, originating from *Phalaenopsis gigantea*, a species which can flower simultaneously with multiple hundreds of flowers. *Phalaenopsis* hybrids are bred from species found in the wild, a good forty of which are known. These are all species which grow in Asia, with the exception of one, which is found in the most extreme north eastern point of Australia. The name *Phalaenopsis* means 'resembling a night moth'. This name was given by explorers when they saw the large white flowers blossoming in the twilight of the ancient forest.

Because *Phalaenopsis* crosses can flower for so long, in a short time they have become the most popular houseplants in Europe. In the Netherlands, which is one of the largest producers of ornamental plants in the world, the *Phalaenopsis* was by far the number one container plant in 2005. In that year, the auction proceeds amounted to more than 140 million euros, which was an increase of 30 per cent on the previous year! In the United States, *Phalaenopsis* has become the second best selling flowering houseplant. In 2005, the wholesale value of the sold plants in that country was estimated at 144 million dollars, but that amount is based only on the turnover of the largest commercial companies, and is therefore a strong underestimation.

Phalaenopsis tetraspis has near white, waxy flowers with a diameter of five to six centimetres that give off a delicate fragrance.

Most *Phalaenopsis* flowers have no scent, but some species do. For example, this is true for *Phalaenopsis violacea* and *P. amboinensis*; these species have served as parents for obtaining the fragrant *Phalaenopsis* crosses. Examples of these hybrids are *Phalaenopsis* 'Sweet Memory', 'Miva Fragrance', and the 'Aromy Stars' series Copperdora, Liodoro, Odorina, Riodoro, Soledoro, and Sunnydoro.

49

p. 50-51: **Phalaenopsis** literally translates as 'moth-like'. >

Orchid fever:
orchid maniacs
and smugglers

In the second half of the twentieth century, orchids became available to everyone. With the new and modern mass propagation techniques, you can buy a whole assortment in any large department store or florist. Many people now also travel to countries where they come directly into contact with orchids growing in the wild. As a result, the number of orchid lovers worldwide has greatly increased. It is estimated that in the USA there are four hundred thousand orchid lovers each with a collection worth more than 500 dollars; globally there are several million people growing orchids.

Some people are so obsessed by these plants that they devote their lives to this passion. Charles Darrow, the inventor of the Monopoly game, retired at the age of forty-six, and dedicated his remaining life completely to orchids. Another example is the founder of Japan Airlines, Michihiro Fukashima. He was so disgusted by the business world that he took early retirement and relocated to Malaysia with his two thousand orchids with which he spent the rest of his life.

There are enthusiasts who are satisfied with the beauty of the commonly available orchids and who like to cultivate hybrids, but there are also collectors who want to possess rare and hard-to-find species at any cost. Rarity is highly prized. With orchids, this usually concerns species that have just been discovered or are hard to cultivate, so that plants have to be taken out of nature. The habitats of newly discovered species are sometimes completely plundered because these plants can be sold at high prices.

In an attempt to protect orchids, they have been incorporated into the Convention on International Trade in Endangered Species (CITES). This is an international treaty for the protection of endangered species. The most well known examples of species protected by this convention are animals, including African elephants, which are killed for their ivory, and rhinoceroses because of the supposed medicinal properties of their horns. This treaty, which has been ratified by more than one hundred countries, limits the trade of these species over international borders. The import of orchids is strictly regulated. Some species are almost entirely banned from export or import (species from CITES Annex 1). Cross border movement is permissible for other species, but only with the required documents. Moreover, a distinction is made between cultivated specimens and those originating from the wild. To import orchids from another country (except between EU countries who have signed the Schengen agreement), it is therefore necessary to apply for documents. Otherwise the plants will be confiscated by the customs service; and those who attempt to import orchids illegally can be sentenced to fines or even imprisonment. The application of CITES laws has already put many orchid smugglers behind bars, but it has also given many orchid growers headaches and problems.

Among the orchids listed in CITES Annex 1 — the most strictly protected species — are the Lady's Slippers of the genus *Paphiopedilum*. All such species are very popular with orchid lovers (some are therefore sold for hundreds or even thousands of euros). Most are now rare in the wild, in a number of cases because all the known habitats have been plundered to gather plants for sale. The case of *Paphiopedilum vietnamense*, discovered in Vietnam in 1997, is particularly distressing, as it would have become extinct

Odontoglossum charlesworthii x refulcis has bright red or orange flowers. >

Paphiopedilum lowii var. richardianum developes three to
seven flowers per stem.

from the mass collection of the plants from its only known
habitat. In 1989, all species of this genus were placed on
Annex 1 of CITES. However, this has not prevented some
people from trying to collect plants anyway or smuggle
them over borders.

At the end of 1987 the orchid collector Henry
Azadehdel was arrested at Heathrow Airport for smuggling.
He was alternately depicted in the press as a smuggler, re-
searcher or semi-official advisor on orchids for the Royal
Botanic Gardens at Kew. Azadehdel had made several jour-
neys to Southeast Asia in the eighties, from which he
brought back rare orchids, usually *Paphiopedilum* species.
He maintained close relations with Kew Gardens and even

had one species of Lady's Slipper named after him, *Paphiopedilum henryanum*. Azadehdel was caught at Heathrow
trying to import thirteen seedlings of *Phragmipedium besseae*, when they were still on the Appendix-II lists without
having the required papers (both CITES and a plant-health
certificates). Subsequently, Azadehdel's house was searched
and about a hundred orchids were seized. He was given a
prison sentence and fined more than 30,000 dollars.

In 1995, an Indonesian orchid grower was sentenced to five months in prison for smuggling hundreds of
Paphiopedilum plants to the United States, while in 2006, Dr.
Sian Tiong Lim, then head of the research department of a
pharmaceutical company in London, was sentenced to four

months. He was caught at Heathrow Airport with hundreds of orchids from Malaysia, including plants of *Paphiopedilum rothschildianum, P. sanderianum,* and *Paphiopedilum gigantifolium,* a species first discovered in 1997 on the island of Sulawesi, and supposedly extinct in its original location. Dr. Lim was a fervent orchid collector, who had imported thousands of plants for resale within a couple of years.

Much has been said and written regarding CITES legislation and its enforcement, and it is certain that in some cases it has led to excesses. This has caused as much irritation for the (professional) growers as for researchers. Within the orchid world, the story of botanist Dr. Guido Braem and the German customs is well known. For the editorial of a book on Paphiopedilums, he sent a flower pickled in alcohol to Germany. This had been collected in 1905 underthe (invalid) name *Cypripedium schmidtianum.* Braem wanted to research this flower in order to be able to ascertain to which *Paphiopedilum* species it actually belonged; he had been lent the flower by the botanical institute of Copenhagen. Since it concerned a loan, the flower in the bottle of alcohol had been sent without invoice or shipment bill. Moreover, no one had thought of applying for CITES permits. When Braem went to collect the bottle with the flower, he was accused of smuggling a protected orchid, transgressing the CITES laws and tax evasion because there was no accompanying invoice. When he declared that it was a loan and that it was for free, the customs officer answered that he did not believe it, because nothing in this world is for free. He tried to explain to the customs officer that the CITES legislation was intended for the protection of live plants, but the customs officer maintained his position that the laws mentioned 'orchids' and not specifically 'live orchids'. After a heated discussion lasting over an hour, the temperamental researcher lost his patience and hit the customs officer in the face. Of course the complaints against him were increased by a charge of assault on an official during the exercise of his post. Finally Dr. Braem got away with a donation of 800 German marks to the local Red Cross department and the charges were revoked. The orchid in question was sent back to Denmark and the researcher then made the journey himself to study this flower.

The same botanist experienced something similar with dried orchids which he had sent from the Reichenbach Herbarium of the Natural History Museum of Vienna. The herbarium specimens were seized, and the director of

The flowers of **Gongora truncata** are hanging down.

the Museum had to involve the Austrian government in order to retrieve them. The fact that a scientist can experience so many problems with CITES in the course of their research may seem amazing. It is entirely possible within the regulations for researchers to obtain a 'CITES scientific permit', when the import of plans for scientific or educative purposes is at stake. However, this is only applicable when plants are shipped by mutual agreement between scientific institutions, and not in the case of independent researchers, such as Dr. Braem, who was not connected to any such institution at that time. Furthermore, according to some researchers it depends on which institution one works for, as some institutions seem to be 'more equal' than others under the law.

Gunnar Seidenfaden was a Danish botanist, world famous as an expert on orchids from Thailand and Northeast Asia. He himself had contributed to the refinement of CITES regulations from the beginning. The legislation was originally intended for animals and was fine tuned in that context, but a couple of weeks before the convention it was suddenly decided to include plants. Unfortunately, there was no time to work out specific rules for plants, and for a long time they were subjected to the same rules as animals. As a researcher, Seidenfaden encountered frequent difficulties because plants sent to him were seized. This was because the Danish government had not deemed it necessary to provide waivers to the CITES rules for scientists. In a letter directed to the chairman of the IUCN World Conservation Union Orchid Specialist Group in 1992, he wrote that 'CITES has developed into a bureaucratic police force, dominated by lawyers with an obsession for formalistic hair splitting and juridical subtleties, who have absolutely no understanding of plants'.

Orchid growers have also had nasty experiences with the import of plants from foreign countries. It has happened frequently that consignments of orchids have been seized by customs because the documents did not appear to be in order, or because plants had not been cultivated, according to experts, but had come straight from the wild. The most spectacular incident was probably the invasion by a police raid commando with automatic weapons and dogs on a German nursery in 1988. They were accompanied by international experts who indicated which plants were illegal. The action took a whole day and night and part of the following day. In total almost eight thousand containers with plants were seized and taken away in trucks. The cultivator Bosha Popow never saw the plants again, and there were several rumours as to what had happened to them. Numerous plants taken in by plant gardens would have possibly died due to negligence and taxed plants would have surfaced in commercial companies abroad. Popow was accused of smuggling orchids and the public prosecutor requested an imprisonment of two years and a fine of 750,000 German marks. Ultimately, Popow was not sentenced for any crime, but nonetheless fined 10,000 marks.

Unfortunately, there have also been incidents where the importer had the required CITES documents, but the orchids were still seized and the importer was accused

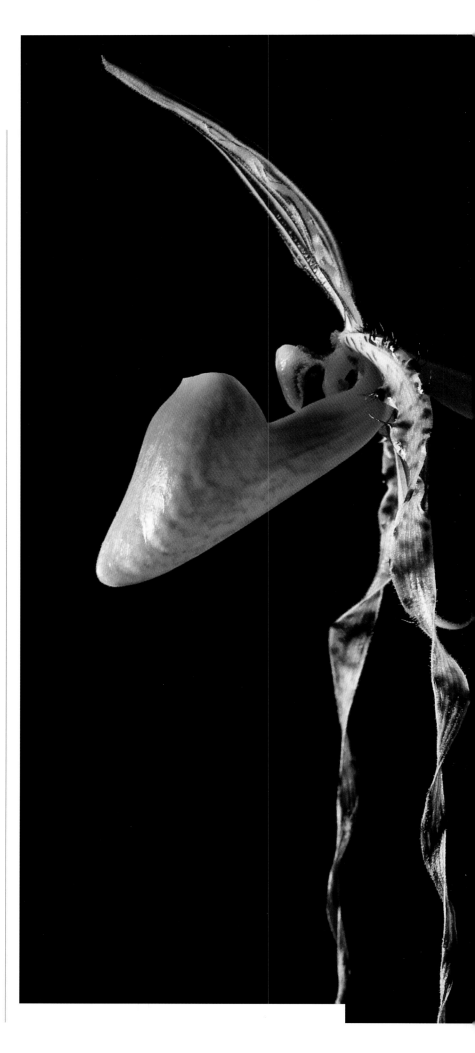

Paphiopedilum rothschildianum x sanderianum

of smuggling. This happened to Kerry Richards, the owner of the orchid nursery Limericks Inc. in Florida. He had imported Chinese cultivated orchids with all the necessary documents including the CITES import permit provided in Cantonese. A couple of months after their import into the USA the cultivator decided to take a portion of these plants to the orchid exhibit in Newbury, England. However, the English government refused to provide a CITES import permit for these plants, based on the fact that all Chinese Paphiopedilums were illegal. According to them, the Chinese authorities had never provided CITES permits and they concluded that these documents must be false. Richards contacted the American Department of Fishing and Conservation (which is qualified for CITES), to have the authenticity of his original Chinese import permit affirmed. However, there the officials questioned whether the CITES office in Canton was authorised to issue an export permit. To resolve this situation the orchid grower addressed the secretariat of the CITES organisation in Geneva, which confirmed that the office in Canton was genuinely authorised. However, in the end he was not granted the import licence for importing his plants to the United Kingdom. Even worse was the fact that several months later employees from the American Department for Fishing and the Environment came to confiscate all Paphiopedilums from the Chinese consignment in his nursery. The validity of his CITES import licence, which they had accepted at first, was once again called into question. According to them, the licence had been tampered with.

There are probably no orchid growers who have never had to deal with any problems related to CITES. Even the famous French grower Marcel Lecoufle, descendant of the family of the reputable Etablissements Lecoufle in Boissy-Saint-Léger near Paris, was implicated. In 1989, the company had acted in good faith when it bought some *Paphiopedilum* plants from a Philippine nursery without thinking to ask for his CITES papers. After all, this wasn't an import, the plants had already been brought through French customs, and their inspectors were also present at the exhibition. Two years later, Lecoufle was visited by a lady who was interested in the Paphiopedilums and asked where they had come from. He told her the full story quite innocently, but it turned out later that this visitor reported him. A customs raid was carried out at his nursery and inspectors seized approximately four hundred plants, which were taken to botanical gardens where unfortunately most of them died within a few years.

Due to numerous such incidents, some people claim that the CITES regulations tend to make life difficult for honest and law-abiding people, while the criminals simply do not care about the rules. The prices of eagerly sought after species actually increased after the Convention came into force, making smuggling much more profitable. A challenge for the enforcement of the law is that it is very difficult to identify orchids, especially when they are not in bloom, and plants have been imported under a false name more than once. More fundamental criticism of CITES is based on the fact that generally there are too few hard facts to confirm the claim that the orchid trade constitutes a real threat to certain species in the wild. The exact quantities of plants found nowadays are difficult to calculate. Some people even say that these laws only provide protection against conditions prevalent in the nineteenth century which are no longer applicable. In any case, the fact is that the legislation involves a lot of administrative rigmarole and in some countries it is only possible to obtain licences by giving bribes to the right people. Finally, there is criticism aimed at CITES because it is now virtually impossible to save orchids by lawful means when their habitat is threatened, for example, when a rain forest is felled or roads, dams, or golf courses are built. Developing land for agriculture and mine construction are major reasons why some species of orchids are disappearing, however, these are usually considered well within the law.

< **Paphiopedilum armeniacum** has splendid yellow flowers.

Orchids in art and literature

The elegant **Cymbidium goeringii** is the most common orchid depicted in traditional Chinese painting.

Orchids have been a favourite subject in Chinese art since the time of the Sung dynasty (960-1279 A.D.). The simplicity and elegance of *Cymbidium* leaves and flowers have made them an ideal subject for both brush drawings and calligraphy. Tjang Bian-Kwiu, a high ranking army officer in the 18th century resigned his post to dedicate the rest of his life to this kind of brush painting and poetry. The most common orchid in traditional brush art of that time was the elegant *Cymbidium goeringii*, of which the variety Tjoe-en Kim means "Spring sword". This orchid was called the 'Chun Lan' or 'Spring Orchid'.

In Japanese painting, images of flowers belong to a category of work known as Kachôga. In this genre, flowers are generally depicted together with birds, a tradition actu-ally derived from Chinese painting and introduced in Japan during the Muromachi period (15th and 16th centuries). Here, the genre developed into a symbolic and poetic art, which interprets the chafing melancholia of things (mono no aware). A classic form was the Shikunshi (the four plants) which depicted the orchid, bamboo, East Indian cherry (*Prunus*), and chrysanthemum. Orchids were also frequently the subject of poems in the East. In his poem about orchids, 'Leaves', Zhang Yu (1333-1385) writes: "Glistening of the dew, and in large disorder they bend themselves, as moved by the wind." He also writes: "The sight of the leaves thrilled me more than the sight of flowers."

Meanwhile, orchids were mentioned only sporadi-cally in ancient Western literature; where they were, it was in

Cypripedium fasciolatum is a big-flowered Venus Shoe from southern China.

the context of their alleged properties to stimulate love. The use of orchids by prostitutes was described briefly in 'Satyricon', a tale written by the Roman Petronius in the first century B.C.

During the middle ages in Europe, orchids were sometimes depicted on tapestries, albeit rather rarely and never just as background, but always with a symbolic meaning. One of the world's most famous tapestries is 'The Captured Unicorn', made sometime around the year 1500 by unknown weavers. It is part of a series of wall tapestries called 'The Hunting of the Unicorn', and was in possession of the influential French family de la Rochefoucauld for centuries. The series was bought by John Rockefeller Jr., and given to the Metropolitan Museum of Art in New York, where it is now kept in The Cloisters in Manhattan. This tapestry was made originally as a wedding present. The unicorn symbolises the bridegroom captured by the bride. Right in front of the unicorn, in the middle of the composition, there is a shining orchid in bloom, intended to bring the married couple good fortune and high fertility.

During the nineteenth century, orchid cultivation developed into a pastime for the rich, and had equal footing with horse racing, hunting, and art collecting. Yet it was not until the second half of that century that orchids became a common subject for art and literature. These often bizarre and eccentric flowers strongly tickled the human imagination and orchids became naturalised in the collective conscience as a symbol of demoralisation or evil, or at least as repulsive flowers. In 1856, 'L'Oiseau' by Jules Michelet describes orchids thus: "On the barks of giant trees hang these fantastic orchids, the beloved daughters of fever, stained children of air, bizarre vegetable butterflies, and they seem to fly. In this fatal loneliness, they twist themselves in stinking emanations and they drink death which gives them life; they show by the whims of their unbelievable colours the intoxication of nature". In the novel 'A Rebours' (Paris 1884) J.K. Huysmans describes Paphiopedilums as flowers with complex and even incoherent shapes, seemingly designed by a crazy inventor. "They look like a clog, from which a curled up human tongue shines, as in images of books which reflect sicknesses of the throat and mouth."

In England, orchids were viewed much in the same way. John Ruskin, a prominent art critic of his day, applauded domestic flowers, which grew wildly in hedgerows and fields and which he considered to be much more beautiful than flowers cultivated in greenhouses and official gardens. He admired the pure and perfect symmetry of roses and poppies, but he found orchids sensual, repulsive, distorted, and imperfect, and in their bizarre shapes he even detected a devilish influence. According to him the *Cypripedium* looked more like the shoes of deformed dwarfs with gout than the shoes of ladies, and he described the parts of some orchids as the stuck-out tongue of an old fool. In his book 'Proserpina' (1875-1886), he pleaded for the name 'orchids' to be replaced by 'Ophrids', which is derived from the Greek word for eyebrow. After all, this would sound more distinguished than the current name, which is derived from 'orchis', the Greek word for testicle!

When Oscar Wilde's novel 'The Portrait of Dorian Gray' appeared in 1890, praising the beauty of orchids more than once, the species received even more condemnation. According to one eminent person, the beauty such as embodied by orchids was a sin in England. Wilde was regarded by Victorian moralists as the high priest of decadence. According to contemporary public opinion, orchids were even associated with homosexuality. By the start of the twentieth century, the shapes of orchids were regarded as grotesque and the word 'orchidaceaous' described flamboyant and immoral behaviour. It was linked to a certain exoticism and some English authors even associated them with the French, who were called degenerate and repulsive.

In France itself, the famous novel by Marcel Proust, 'Du côté de chez Swann', appeared in 1913. In this tale, a *Cattleya* flower becomes the symbol of the sexual relationship which the main character maintains with the courtesan Odette de Crécy. At their first meeting, one of the *Cattleyas* which she wears on her corset comes off and he helps her to put it back on. From that time onwards, 'to do Cattleya' means to make love. Orchids have frequently been associated with sexuality. Elsewhere in European literature, orchids have also been used to depict the darker side of erotica and forbidden impulses. In the book 'Orchideen: Sonderbare Geschichten', which appeared in 1905, the German writer Meyerink wrote some bizarre stories related to witchcraft, alchemy, Eastern magic, astronomy, and all sorts of mysterious matters. The story 'Tears of Bologna' tells of the Orchid Queen Mercedes, a witch with red hair and green eyes, who seduced and destroyed a certain Tonio. In this book, orchids are a symbol of beauty which serves evil. Here is a short extract from this book: "Orchids are actually not flowers at all, but satanic creatures, beings which merely show us the horns of their shape, and show us their eyes, lips, and tongues, in a sensual seductive twirl of colours, so that we would not suspect that terrible adder body which hides itself (invisibly and bringing death) in the realms of shadow." Some people would be afraid of much less!

In the same period, fantastic horror stories were written about orchids, such as in the story 'The Flowering of the Strange Orchid' (1894) by H.G. Wells. According to this tale, an orchid lover (a bachelor) buys some orchids at an auction in London which have just been imported from the Andaman Islands. For the orchid hunter who had collected them, it was his last trip because he had been found dead in a marsh with all the blood sucked from his body, supposedly by leeches. Thanks to a befriended ornithologist who was with him on this expedition, the orchids were nevertheless brought to England. Amongst the acquisitions of this enthusiast, there was a strange looking orchid, entirely shrivelled and dried out. After some weeks of good care, the plant started to revive forming leaves and long aerial roots with flattened ends. This plant did not look like one of the well-known orchids, so it was therefore a new species. Full of tension and curiosity, the owner waited until the flowers appeared. When the plant finally started to bloom, he hurried to his greenhouse. Immediately, as he comes in, he smells the heavy, sweet fragrance. In ecstasy, he admires the splendid flowers, but becomes captured by the fragrance and everything around him starts spinning. After a while, his landlady becomes worried because he fails to appear for the traditional cup of tea at half past three. She goes to the greenhouse and finds him lying motionless on the ground, with the tentacle-like aerial roots around his neck, on his chin, and on his hands. She stares at all this, and under one of the tentacles she sees blood dripping. Screaming, she rushes towards him and tries to release him from the long tentacles, but she feels herself becoming unwell. She runs quickly to the door and, coming back to her senses, she throws a flower pot through a window to let some fresh air into the greenhouse. Eventually, she is able to release him and thankfully he is still alive. By contrast, the terrible orchid withers, turns black, and dies.

Another gruesome tale is 'The Purple Terror' by White (1899). Discovered on an expedition in the jungles of Cuba, the main character, Will Scarlet, discovers purple orchids with a deep red centre, known as 'poppies of the devil' by the local inhabitants. His first, confusing meeting with the flowers does not take place in the forest, but in a drinking arena, where they shine on the décolleté of a beautiful female dancer. Eventually, our hero succeeds in finding out where they come from and he travels there at once. They appear to grow on giant trees as parasites on a plateau in the mountains, high above the jungle. Under the trees he finds a stack of animal and human bones. Scarlet discovers that the orchids have long tentacles, with which they catch unsuspecting victims at night, and then kill with their thorns.

In visual art, orchids have often been used as a subject in Art Nouveau, amongst other things. One of the prominent artists of this genre was the Frenchman Emile Gallé, who specialised in making glass objects. He developed his own style with opaque glass into which subjects were etched or cut, frequently plants. Gallé had also studied botany in his youth and found inspiration in the wild plants he studied in nature. He considered orchids as strange, sumptuous, capricious, and mysterious, or even alarming. He proclaimed in his native tongue: "We prefer the dear old plants cherished by our ancestors. But the fast, modern stream is deeper and more powerful than the peaceful rivulet of our preferences. It sweeps everything away. It throws us the orchid, as a last bouquet by Ophelia, with a richness, an enigmatic strangeness of varieties, perfumes, colours, whims, desires and disturbing mysteries." These sentences are a component of his official speech 'Le Décor symbolique' that he gave on 17 May 1900 at the Stanislas Academy in Nancy and which contains a sort of profession of faith by the artist. Later, he said he was more sensitive to "the enchantment of the blue hue of periwinkles" than to the "octopus-like gestures of orchids". Despite this reservation, Gallé made several superb creations featuring orchids, both domestic and exotic species such as Paphiopedilums and Cattleyas. The vase 'Les Lumineuses' was made by Emile Gallé on the occasion of the World Exhibition in Paris in 1900, and is now part of the collection of the Museum für Kunst und Gewerbe in Hamburg. Gallé also made some artistically adorned pieces of furniture and often used orchids as decoration, as for the chest of drawers 'Les orchidées et les insectes', which was made for the World Exhibition of 1889.

At the start of the twentieth century, orchids were becoming associated with rich and prosperous environments and were considered 'chic', although they always had a sensual aura. In Hollywood they became a symbol of passion in the jungle or other exotic locations. In 1929, the silent movie 'Wild Orchids' was shown, in which Greta Garbo plays the neglected wife of a businessman on Java (Indonesia) who falls in love with a handsome young Javanese prince. Both lovers carried orchids in the film. Four years later came the film 'Flying down to Rio' with Fred Astaire and Ginger Rogers playing the leading roles. This was about the forbidden passion of a musician who falls in love with a beautiful lady on a Brazilian island and composes the song 'Orchids in the Moonlight' for her "because she is an orchid".

Rather different are the novels in which detective Nero Wolfe has to solve all kinds of murder cases; this series was produced between 1934 and 1968. The main character has a splendid orchid collection, so in these books orchids are frequently referred to by name. It is clear from the books that the writer, Rex Stout, was himself an orchid fanatic. Indeed, according to his next of kin, he spent at least four hours with his orchids every day and called them his concubines. In the novel 'Black Orchids' (1941), the detective leaves his New York residence to look for a black orchid in a

This elegant vase 'Les Lumineuses' was made by the artist Emile Gallé for the world exhibition in Paris in 1900. It now resides at the Museum für Kunst und Gewerbe in Hamburg.

flower show, but gets involved in the search for a murderer. Another best seller is the book 'No Orchids for Miss Blandish', written in 1939 by James Hadley Chase. This focuses on a beautiful virgin daughter of a millionaire in Kansas City, who is brutally kidnapped and violated by a gangster. However, she falls in love with her kidnapper and ends up taking her own life. Critics labelled the book as immoral and sadistic, and the subsequent film was banned by the censors.

In contemporary literature, orchids also appear as a symbol of feelings that are not at all associated with darkness. The autobiographical novel 'Orquideas: desplumando un milagro' by Y. Panoutsos (2002) was dedicated to "all 'orchids' which have made life beautiful and relieve us from the heavy shadows which weigh on all men. These are orchids such as mothers, sisters, fiancées, lovers, wives, and girlfriends. They are blessed!" Another example is the 'Metaphysical Orchids', a play written in 2001 by the Spanish Antonio Leandro Garcia-Calderon y Ponce. In this piece, a man gives orchids to his wife who is in labour "to accompany you when I am not at your side". The woman tells her new-born son that she wants the orchids which she has received from his father to be for him. "My heart wants them to be transformed into metaphysical orchids for you, invisible and without shapes, as abstract flowers; thoughts, dreams, good desires, fortune, peace, and all good things for you." All her life, his mother gives him orchids, which acquire a particular meaning for him as an adult man. "The strange shape of the flowers, their splendid colours, their decorative impact, the difficulty in cultivating them, and the long period that they remain fresh made me consider orchids as a symbol of spirituality, but also of practical reality, because we live in a world of tangible matter, activity, and progress."

In the field of contemporary visual art, the orchid works of painter John Thomas represent a separate style. This American, who lived in Hawaii for a long time and died there in 2003, made extraordinary compositions of orchids with watercolours. He painted scenes from Hawaiian legends, and his art was also influenced by Italian Renaissance and Gestalt psychology. Thomas' work has been circulated in many private and public art collections, such as in the Hirschhorn collection in the Smithsonian Museum of International and Contemporary Art in Washington DC. The book 'Orchid Art and the Orchid Isle' gives a beautiful overview of his drawings and paintings, which are presented together with poems by Harvey Hess.

Another artist who was inspired by orchids is Tomi Ungerer. He is especially known for his social satirical drawings, his drawings for children's books, but also his erotic drawings (these three categories have, however, appeared in separate books). In 1988, 'Tomi Ungerer's Botanik' was published, with drawings of erotically charged flowers like *Cypripedium* (Lady Slipper). The caption for this drawing is "Lady slipper, lonely and stranded, hairless scrotum of the forest, well! You can't have everything." He also made drawings of imaginary flowers like a completely pink 'Orchis clitto erectus', which leaves little to the imagination!

Orchids between
heaven
and
earth

For some people, orchids also have a mystical meaning and they have certainly found a place within the New Age movement. In the book 'Orchids and Mandalas — the Quantum Healing of the Universe' (2006) R. Martinez Lopez explains why. According to Eastern philosophy, the universe consists solely of energy, which is constantly moving. Like all living organisms, orchids possess an energy level that makes them vibrate with a certain frequency. Orchids are supposed to vibrate with a frequency of 100 to 200 Megahertz, depending on the species and its habitat. The epiphytic orchids, which grow high in the trees are said to possess a higher frequency than terrestrial types. The vibration energy of orchids is a lot higher than that of the human body, which purportedly vibrates at 50 MHz, and the human brain, which vibrates with a frequency of 80 MHz. Due to their high vibration, it is believed that orchids can be used as medicine for many kinds of disorders. The Theory of Bach states that plants have healing properties because of their ultrasound energy. Edward Bach was a Welsh doctor who lived from 1886 to 1936. In his view, illness arises because of an emotional imbalance, caused by a conflict between the personality and the soul, which forms the essence of every person. Because of these theories, he is considered to be a forerunner in the holistic health movement. According to Bach, flowers cause feelings, and these feelings result in bodily responses, both in the immune and the hormonal system, as well as the nervous system. He developed 38 medicines based on flowers of several European plant varieties, the so-called Bach Flower Remedies. These are said to contain the energy extract of the flowers.

The Theory of Bach is partly derived from the old Celtic belief, which proclaimed that plants are mediators between the earth and the sun. Flowers form the passage or link between life and death, because they form seeds which are apparently dead, but pass on life. This belief explains the fact that the Holy Grail, known to us from the legend of King Arthur and the Knights of the Round Table, was symbolised as a kettle full of flowers. It would have the power to raise the dead and to heal those wounded by life. Similar conceptions existed as early as the time of the Olmecs, a nation which lived in Southern and Central Mexico for approximately 1,200 years up to 400 B.C.

In accordance with the Theory of Bach, all sorts of plant extracts have been manufactured in different parts of the world. 'Energy extracts' are now also made from orchids which are supposed to contain healing properties. In this context, orchids are regarded as the queens of the plant world because they possess the highest energy level within the plant realm, especially epiphytic orchids. Since these orchids grow to a height of several metres above the ground, they are supposed to vibrate at the same level as angels. They establish a connection between human beings, the cosmos, and the earth and bring us into contact with different levels of cosmic love. Epiphytic orchids are also supposed to correspond with the five higher 'chakras' of the spiritual body, while terrestrial orchids possess a lower level of energy corresponding to the lower chakras. A chakra is a centre of activity which receives, assimilates, and expresses vital energy in accordance with the Eastern Vedic tradition. Although chakras are not material entities, they occupy a certain position in relation to the human body. Certain chakras are also associated with different levels of consciousness and spirituality. Since orchids are considered to be situated at the highest spiritual level, they are supposed to be able to bring us up to a higher level of consciousness. Orchids can connect the rational to the emotional within us, likewise the consciousness to the subconscious, and the past to the future.

Pleione Yunnanensis >

p. 68-69: **Scaphosepalum merinoi** comes from Ecuador and was first described in 2002.

II

Orchids as seducers

a story of seduction

Everything
you ever wanted to know about
orchid sex

Orchids cannot take care of their own reproduction. After all, plants are not capable of meeting a partner since it is impossible for them to move. For sexual reproduction to take place, firstly flowers have to be available since they are the sex organs of plants. Sex organs provide for the creation of new creatures that have an original combination of characteristics from a male and female parent. The new combinations of characteristics that are created make it possible for individuals of the same species to have considerable differences, so that there is more chance of producing one or more individuals suitable for adapting to a constantly changing environment. A second requirement for sexual reproduction in plants is pollination. This is the moment when grains of pollen containing the male seed cells arrive on the stigma, which is a part of the flower's female organs. The stigma is sticky and is connected by the style to the female egg cells inside the ovary. If everything goes well the grains of pollen grow like a tube inside the style to the egg cells, where they present the male seed cells to the egg cells so that fertilisation can occur and seeds can be formed. Most flowers produce individual grains of pollen that are transported by the wind, or some other carrier such as bees, in different directions. Because there are so many individual grains there is a considerable chance that a number of them will find their way to receptive female flowers.

The individuality of orchids primarily comes from a shared flower structure. They have six petals, as do the related lilies and tulips. With tulips, the three outer petals (the sepals) are the same as the inner petals, which are enclosed in bud. With orchids the inner petals are generally different to the outer petals (sepals), but what is particularly striking is that one inner petal is formed completely differently to all the other petals. This is known as the lip, or labellum, and it generally differs from the other petals in colour, form and/or size. The lip is important for the pollination of orchids since it generally functions as a landing platform on which the pollinating insects can land. The 'column' is located above the lip. This is a structure with a hood on its tip under which the male pollinia lie, with the stigma, the receptive female organ, underneath.

In contrast with other plants, most orchids don't produce separate grains of pollen but instead have lumps of pollen grains (pollinia) that stay glued together. These are generally found on a small stalk (up to 1.6 cm long) that has a very sticky, small disc on its tip. If you touch this small disc with your finger it will quickly stick. If a pollinator, generally an insect, touches the small disc the pollinia will stick to its body, on its head or abdomen for example. If the insect then flies to a different flower and comes in contact with the stigma, it will leave the pollinia behind.

Since orchid pollen is transferred in one go it is a case of all or nothing. Each flower has only one chance to pollinate another. This is also probably the reason why many orchid flowers take a long time to wilt, sometimes over three months. The record for the longest flowering orchid is probably held by *Grammatophyllum multiflorum* that can remain in flower for as long as nine months. Nevertheless, there are orchids whose flowers only stay open for a day or even less: the record goes to *Dendrobium appendiculatum*, whose flowers only stay open for five minutes! With some species the flowers never open because no external pollinator is needed: the flower is self-pollinated (pollen from the same flower is used for the pollination).

72

One of the six petals of **Chysis bractescens**, from Mexico, has a different >
colour and shape than the other ones and is called the lip.

In the middle of the flower is the column which contains pollinia on top.

Self-pollination is however a lot less common in orchids than cross-pollination, where pollen is delivered from a different plant. Cross-pollination creates a unique combination of genetic material. It offers a greater chance of survival than self-pollination where the descendants are in principle genetically identical to the parent. Cross-pollination provides the big advantage of an increased likelihood of individuals among the descendants with varying characteristics, better equipped to face the challenges of an ever-changing world. But cross-pollination has its price: cross-pollination requires a carrier, preferably from other plants, to transport the pollen to different flowers. It therefore costs more effort and energy to achieve cross-pollination.

Most orchids therefore need the help of creatures, often insects, for their pollination. They are pollinated by bees, bumblebees, wasps, butterflies, flies, moths and even by birds. In order to tempt pollinators the orchid has to first attract their attention. This is initially achieved by the flowers' colour: the more striking the better. The visual seduc-

Dendrochilum cobbianum has flowers of only one to two centimetres. >
These have a delicate fragrance reminiscent of freshly mown grass.

tiveness of each colour is different however, and this depends on the species of pollinators that are attracted. Colours are perceived differently by these animals according to the species that they belong to.

A second way to attract pollinators is by using scent. A lot of orchids have evolved to tempt specific insects with the scent of their flowers. These fragrances can be pleasant to the human nose but those used to entice flies are not surprisingly unpleasant. A few examples of the diverse scents produced by orchids are: vanilla, violets, orange blossom, the heavy, sweet scent of heliotrope, jasmine, lilies of the valley, almonds, honey, hyacinth, mint, leather, cinnamon, dried hay, fungi, algae, fish, rotting flesh and faeces.

Once the flower's colour and smell have caught the attention of potential pollinators, they also have to be convinced that there is something to be gained from the flower. Most flowers offer a reward in exchange for a pollinator's visit, either in the form of pollen or as nectar that they can use as food. We know honeybees for example, collect pollen and bring it to their nest as food for their larvae. However, the pollen from most orchids can't be used for this because it is glued together. Honeybees do however, collect nectar which they use to make honey. Nectar is a sweet liquid that plants produce and offer in the flowers or other parts of the plant. It is also the substance that butterflies suck up when they drink from a flower with their proboscis.

Even though there are numerous examples of orchid species that are visited by just one species of pollinator, there are also a lot of species that can be pollinated by numerous creatures from different groups. These orchids generally produce nectar.

The production of nectar requires an awful lot of the plant's energy, according to some calculations, between 3-30% of its total energy supply! In order to save energy some orchids have developed tricks to tempt pollinators without offering nectar. Approximately one third of all species do not produce nectar. These orchids have developed different strategies in order to continue to tempt creatures without exchanging nectar or pollen. One of these is mimicry, which means imitation, where the flowers look like other flowers that do produce nectar. For example, the flowers of *Cymbidium insigne* and *Dendrobium infundibulum* orchids that grow in the North of Thailand have flowers that look exactly like those of *Rhododendron lyi*, a species that occurs in the same region. The trio is pollinated by the same kind of bumblebee. Some orchids imitate species that offer pollen. In order to make the deception more realistic their flowers have small, round, yellow hairs that mimic pollen. Still others spread the smell of nectar without actually offering it. However, there is also sexual mimicry where orchids tempt male insects by imitating the females. To put it briefly, there are an awful lot of examples of orchids that achieve pollination by fooling other creatures!

Just how orchids won their reputation as the masters of seduction is explained in the following chapters. Examples are given of the often complicated strategies and tricks that orchids use to ensure reproduction. First we discuss Charles Darwin, the father of evolutionary theory, who was one of the first to discover the link between the construction and appearance of flowers and the method of pollination. After this there are chapters about pollination by bees and wasps, flies, butterflies, moths and birds respectively.

< Five of the six petals of the related species, **Chysis aurea,** are white at the base and orangey-bronze at the top. The flower's lip is speckled and spotted on the inside.

Charles Darwin

and the Theory of

Evolution

Charles Darwin is particularly known for his theory of evolution, a milestone in science, which he introduced to the world in 1859. The first edition of his book 'On the Origin of Species' sold out on the day of publication. At the age of twenty-two Darwin sailed around the world for five years on the sailing ship 'The Beagle' making scientific observations. His observations concerning matters that included the species of finches on the Galapagos Islands, led him to formulate his ideas concerning the origin of species which were revolutionary in those times and were regarded as heretical by many. The theory of evolution is still contested today by what are known as creationists, religiously inspired people who firmly believe in the story of the Creation as it is presented in the Bible. Darwin illustrated his theory of evolution with observations of orchids among other things. In 1862 he wrote the book "The various contrivances by which orchids are fertilised by insects". In this volume he made the link between the form and structure of orchid flowers and their pollinators. Darwin based his studies on orchid flowers because of the abundance of ingenious mechanisms they use to ensure that pollination is achieved. In contrast with a lot of other flowers, orchids are not radially symmetric but bilaterally symmetric, which is to say that they can only be mirrored by one plane of symmetry. This indicates greater specialisation in pollination. Radially symmetric flowers can be pollinated by all sorts of different insects who can do this in a variety of positions, but bilaterally symmetrical flowers generally have a limited group of possible pollinators and sometimes just one or two species. With orchids, the position of the pollinator at the moment of pollination is crucially important because their pollen grains are glued together to form one or two pollinia. It demands impressive precision for the pollinia to be placed in the correct position so that the pollinator will leave them behind on the stigma of another flower. Perfect positioning of the pollinia is essential and orchids have developed astoundingly precise mechanisms

for this purpose over the course of evolution. Darwin consequently wrote in his book that the study of the numerous, beautiful, pollination mechanisms used by orchids would generate a lot more popular respect for the plant world.

How these precise mechanisms work can be illustrated by referring to Darwin's findings concerning the indigenous European orchid *Anacamptis pyramidalis*, the Pyramidal Orchid. This species is visited by butterflies that use their long proboscis to extract nectar from the flower's spur, a tubular structure on the labellum that is closed at the bottom. There are two ridges at the entrance to this tube that force the butterfly to insert its proboscis in the correct position to attach the sticky base of the pollinia. This is equipped with flaps that curl around the proboscis so that the stem becomes stuck around the proboscis, or as was the case in Darwin's experiments, a needle. After fifteen seconds the small stem bends so that the pollinia turn ninety degrees, at which point they are in the perfect position for pollinating the next flower the butterfly visits.

By carrying out all kinds of experiments and making precise observations Darwin was able to demonstrate the function of small details in the structures of orchid flowers. What was impressive was that he made predictions that turned out to be accurate. For example, he predicted that the Comet or Star of Bethlehem Orchid, *Angraecum sesquipedale*, a white flowering species from Madagascar, had to be pollinated by a large moth with a thirty centimetre long proboscis. This prediction was based on the fact that this orchid has white flowers and a spur of this length

78

Angraecum germinyanum, a species from Madagascar, mainland Africa, Comoros Island and Sri Lanka >
where they occur up to a height of 2000 meters; it is related to Angraecum sesquipedale, the Comet Orchid.

Cyrtochilum macranthum var. williamsianum grows in the Andean
mountains from Ecuador to Peru at a height of 3000 to 3500 meters.
An individual plant can have as many as five flower stems holding
over a hundred large flowers.

with nectar only present at the lowest level. White flowers generally indicate pollinators that are active at night since such flowers are most visible then. The pollinators are often moths that have a proboscis, which they use to extract the nectar. The nectar is generally present in what is known as the spur, a long, hollow tube. However, in the case of *Angraecum sesquipedale*, the spur was longer than the proboscis of all known moths and Darwin consequently asserted that there must be a moth with a longer proboscis on Madagascar. Numerous scholars greeted this idea with howls of derision. Forty years later, after Darwin's death, a moth was actually found that had a proboscis that was between 30-35 cm long. This insect was *Xanthopan morgani praedicta*, and Darwin received posthumous acknowledgement. This is a textbook example of what is known as co-evolution where both the flower and pollinator have evolved together so that they are perfectly adapted to each other.

Almost all species of *Angraecum* are pollinated by moths, but on La Réunion island, which is a French overseas territory in the Mascarene Archipelago, there are three species that differ from the rest. They have a short, wide spur and do not produce scent during the evening. In 2006 French researchers found that they weren't pollinated by moths but by birds of the species *Zosterops borbonicus* or White-eye Bird. These birds have a short, triangular beak that just fits in the spur of these orchids' flowers. The White-eyes are small, active birds that often extract nectar from flowers and have a specially formed tongue for this purpose. The La Réunion White-eye is perfectly adapted to the *Angraecum striatum* orchid, and the reverse is also true, the result of long-term co-evolution.

Moths are subdivided into two groups, the phalena type (Noctuidae family) that land on flowers to extract nectar and the Sphingidae family, such as the Hummingbird Hawk-Moth, that can remain hovering in the air while extracting nectar. The lip on orchid flowers that are pollinated by the last group is curled up so that insects cannot land on it. Orchids pollinated by moths occur in striking numbers in Africa, but they are also found in other tropical regions. The American species *Epidendrum nocturnum* and *Epidendrum parkinsonianum* have large, star-shaped flowers that have a beautiful scent at night, the second of these smelling of orange blossom. There are also examples closer to home of species that are pollinated by moths such as those of the *Platanthera* genus, which includes *P. bifolia*, the fragrant night orchid that is found throughout Europe and in parts of Asia.

A bee in the bonnet

Approximately sixty percent of all orchids are pollinated by bees, wasps or bumblebees. These include a considerable number from temperate regions that are visited by social bees. These are species of bee that live in organised societies but do not include *Apis mellifera*, the true honeybee. In the tropics in both Asia and America, bees of the *Xylocopa* genus often pollinate orchids. These are large, strong bees that have similarities to bumblebees. These species sometimes 'cheat' by obtaining the nectar without carrying out pollination. In order to do this they bite a hole in the side of the flower at the spot where the nectar is present. In this way they don't follow the traditional route, but plunder nectar without coming in contact with the pollen. The same is done, for that matter, by European bumblebees on the flowers of different plants such as foxgloves (*Digitalis*). Certain orchids have developed hardened plant parts where the nectar is present so that the bumblebees or *Xylocopa* bees can't bite through. A different strategy is to have open nectar glands at the place where the bumblebees could break in. This nectar tempts ants to the plant that consequently guard this spot as their source of food and chase away intruders such as bumblebees, thus forcing them to collect the nectar in the way that benefits pollination. The *Sobralia, Barkeria* and *Schomburgkia* are examples of orchids that are all pollinated by large *Xylocopa bees*.

Bees also pollinate Vandas. *Vanda* is a genus that consists of approximately forty-five Asian orchid species that have magnificent flowers and generally a pleasant scent. Vandas form long, hanging root masses and they are often grown hanging in damp locations rather than planted in pots so that the roots can be exposed. They then live on water that is sprayed on their roots. Despite this, Vandas are true drinkers among orchids and they only do well when they have access to a lot of moisture, light and warmth in

The flowers of the Tongue Orchid, **Serapias lingua**, are adapted to tempt bees to stop the night.

particular, as well as good nutrients. Only the blue *Vanda coerulea* does well in cooler conditions since it grows at higher altitudes in the wild. Vandas are used a lot for hybridisation, even with other genera. It is a very popular group of plants, however, they are a little expensive. This is because it's not unusual for them to take up to ten years before they start to flower.

Otoglossum brevifolium is a native of American >
mountain forests where it grows in the canopy of trees.

The flowers of this **Miltoniopsis hybrid** have inherited the striking pink of its wild ancestors. Pollination of its wild relatives is by nocturnal insects.

Flowers pollinated by bees and wasps are not red but generally blue, violet, purple, yellow or white, since these colours are the ones that these insects can see. In addition, they see UV radiation which human eyes are incapable of doing. Flowers visited by bees release a pleasant, sweet scent. This is the case with *Cattleya* and most species of the closely related *Laelia* genus. Other examples are the *Oncidium* genus species. These are mainly known to the general public as hybrids available in large numbers in shops and have numerous yellow flowers that measure one to two centimetres. Nevertheless, there are many more within this Central and South American genus. A large number of the 680 species have yellow and brown flowers but there are also others with white flowers that have striking colouring that varies from pink to red.

A number of *Oncidium* species produce a wax-like structure in certain parts of the flower. These parts reflect UV light, which makes them easily visible to bees. The bees have special combs on their front and middle legs, which

they use to scrape off oil and transfer it to their rear legs. Oil contains many calories and is an ideal food for bee larvae. One of the species that produces oil is *O. ornithorrhynchum*, a species with small pink flowers that has recently become available in garden centres. The white-flowered version is also sometimes available.

Other *Oncidium* species mislead insects in an unusual way, namely by taking advantage of their aggressive tendencies. In certain species of bee the males display strong territorial behaviour. While the females visit flowers, the males diligently protect the surroundings against intruders, chasing away any insects that get too close. Certain *Oncidium* species also occur in their territory. When the wind disturbs these flowers they look like flying insects; at least in the bees' eyes. The male bees think that they are adversaries and attack the flowers. In doing this they touch the flower for a fraction of a second, long enough for pollen to attach to their faces. When they attack the next flower they unconsciously transfer the pollen to the stigma and pollination has been achieved once more! This method of pollination is called pseudo-antagonism or pseudo-trespassing and is rare in the plant kingdom. It occurs in *Oncidium hyphaematicum, O. stipitatum* and *O. planilabre* among others. It is of crucial importance that the bees are in the correct position when they touch the flowers for pollination to occur. The precision required is less than one millimetre, but they hardly ever miss. It isn't clear exactly which part of the flower specifically arouses the insects' aggression.

Odontoglossum is a close relative of *Oncidium*, a genus that often has spectacular flowers pollinated by bees. There are approximately one hundred and forty species from Central and South America, which often grow at high altitudes and consequently prefer rather cool conditions. Some species within this genus have beautiful white flowers such as *Odontoglossum crispum* and *O. nobile* mentioned above. Crossing has produced beautiful red flowers as is the case with *Odontoglossum charlesworthii x refulcis*.

Another related genus is *Cyrtochilum* whose flowers look somewhat like *Oncidium* since they have the same colours (either yellow/brown or orange/lavender, or magenta or pink shades) but they are bigger. What is unusual about these species are the long flower stems that grow, winding like lianas, far into the overgrowth and with hundreds of flowers in bloom at the same time. A few species imitate liana flowers from the Malpighiaceae family. The flowers from these lianas offer a kind of oil to certain bees in exchange for pollination, but the orchid flowers that imitate them give no such reward. This is another form of mimicry or imitation whereby the bees cannot tell the difference and still visit the flowers. They quickly notice the deception and leave, but in the meantime the pollinia have become stuck to their bodies. They fly to new flowers, but again allow themselves to be fooled, thus pollinating the orchid.

Otoglossum is another related genus of which there are twelve species including *Otoglossum harlingii*, which probably imitates *Calceolaria* (Lady's Purse, Slipper Flower) flowers, which offer oil to bees. *Otoglossum brevifolium* originally comes from American mountain forests where it grows high in the trees.

Although many white orchids are pollinated by moths, there are several species in the *Coelogyne* genus that are instead pollinated by bees and wasps. These are gener-

The Butterfly Orchid, **Orchis papilionacea**, can be found in coastal areas of the Mediterranean Sea.

ally found in the Himalayas, for example, *Coelogyne cristata* and *C. corymbosa*. In lower lying areas there are also species with different colours such as *Coelogyne pandurata* from Malaysia and Indonesia, a variety with green flowers with black markings which has the scent of vanilla and cinnamon.

A small, but charming, orchid pollinated by bees is *Macroclinium manabinum*. This has a spherical inflorescence with individual flowers smaller than 1cm. Their fan-like leaves, which are set in, have an uneven surface. This small plant originates from the Ecuadorian coastal province of Manabi. The bees that pollinate this variety do so by carrying the small pollinia glued between their eyes.

In South America there are bees that only fly in the dark at night and some of these also pollinate orchids. The species *Cattleya luteola* is visited by the bee *Melipona flavipennis*, at around 5.30 am, just before sunrise. They pollinate the flowers in just a few minutes. The orchid *Miltoniopsis warczewicsii* (which was previously known as *Miltonia endresii*) is pollinated at about 4.30 am by the bee species *Ptiloglossa ducalis*. Even though it is still dark, the pollinators work extremely efficiently and quickly. Other species of *Miltoniopsis* are also known to be pollinated at night. They all have white or bright pink flowers that give off the most scent just before sunrise. It is conjectured that this is also the work of bees flying at night even though this hasn't been confirmed by observation. It demands strong motivation from plant experts to carry out research at such an early hour!

There are also species among the indigenous European orchids that are pollinated by bees. This is the case with *Orchis papilionacea,* the Butterfly Orchid, for example, which despite its name is pollinated by *Eucera nigrescens* the Southerly Longhorn Bee. This orchid is found in different countries surrounding the Mediterranean Sea. Its name refers to the similarity of its colourful flowers to a butterfly.

The Tongue Orchid, *Serapias lingua,* is also found in Europe and the Mediterranean. This terrestrial orchid is visited by small bees from the *Ceratinidae* family, which use the flowers as hiding places or even as a place to spend the night. The normal nesting place for these insects is in the hollow stems of blackberries. However, every flower forms a small space in which the insects fit exactly. The flowers

Coelogyne corymbosa has flowers with a perfume similar to Iris and grows in the Himalayas at an altitude of between 1700 and 2800 meters.

release a sweet scent and it is known that predominantly male bees visit the flowers. It has been suggested that these orchids are deliberately imitating bees' nests. Each time that they visit a flower the bees get pollinia stuck to them and up to seven pairs of these have been observed on the heads of some insects.

p. 88-89: Bee pollinated orchids have large prominent lips that serve as a landing platform. >
Schomburgkia superbiens spreads its pollen via **Xylocopa** bees. Its remarkable lip has a sharp outlined pattern and protruding ridges that guide these insects to the pollen like the markings on a runway.

Crocodiles, antelopes, octopuses and invisible colours

The genus *Dendrobium* is one of the largest orchid genera and has about nine hundred species. All these originate from Asia and Oceania where they are found from sea level in the tropics up to altitudes of thousands of metres in the Himalayas. Numerous species come from New Guinea where they grow on trees in swamps in inaccessible regions full of mosquitoes and crocodiles. The largest Dendrobiums reach three metres in height, while the smallest is just a few centimetres tall. The leaves of *Dendrobium cucumerinum,* or Cucumber Orchid, are swollen and resemble small cucumbers. These are an adaptation to dry conditions. It is a species that lives high in the trees in East Australia.

Most Dendrobiums are pollinated by bees. The Australian species, *Dendrobium kingianum* and *D. speciosum,* produce aromatic substances collected by social bees for use as a signal pheromone. Pheromones are (transient) substances that are secreted by living organisms, both animals and plants, which are used to communicate messages to their own kind. The most well-known are sex pheromones which attract members of the opposite sex. However, there are also alarm pheromones such as those secreted by aphids when they are attacked, and which urge the others to flee. Another class of pheromones are the substances that ants deposit along the tracks that they go, which unerringly indicate the way that the other ants from their colony have to follow. No GPS needed! Pheromones don't just occur in insects - they are also produced by mammals and reptiles and it seems probable that humans also secrete them. Pheromones are odourless and detected by the vomeronasal organ, located between the nose and the mouth. The existence of sex pheromones in human beings is still subject to discussion. Even though there are studies that indicate that certain substances increase the power of the sexual attractiveness

The Squid Orchid, **Dendrobium spectabile,** has strange flowers that look like tentacles.

of individuals to the opposite sex. However, the interpretation of these results is regarded as controversial in scientific circles. This doesn't restrain commercial companies from selling sex pheromones and recommending them as the magic potion for more sex! Androstenone is generally marketed to men, a substance that has been clearly proven to work in pigs. This is a substance present in the saliva of boars (male pigs) and sold on a commercial scale to farmers so that they can work out when sows are ready for artificial

A man-made hybrid antelope **Dendrobium**.

insemination. In orchids, several species produce substances that are used as pheromones by their pollinators, which are generally insects (see further).

Many species of *Dendrobium* have beautiful flowers on long stems that stay fresh on the plants for months. This is why many of their species, and in particular hybrids, are grown in Asia as cut flowers and exported to Europe. They are mainly crosses based on *Dendrobium phalaenopsis,* a species from tropical Northwest Australia. The flowers are white, rose, violet or purple. These crosses are also available as houseplants, particularly the smaller varieties. Some species of *Dendrobium* are known as Antelope Orchids. These are tropical species that generally have two upright petals twisted like the horns of an antelope. *Dendrobium tangerinum* is an example of an Antelope Orchid. It is a species from New Guinea with orange flowers and a violet veined spot on its lip. Tangerinum means mandarin-coloured, but the colour of the flowers can vary from orange-brown to almost red. The flowers are five to six centimetres in size and live an extremely long time; they can last up to six months.

93

< The golden-yellow flowers of **Dendrobium harveyanum**
have nectar guides invisible to the human eye.

This Antelope Orchid, **Dendrobium tangerinum,** is from New Guinea.

Antelope Orchids are crossed with *Dendrobium phalaenopsis*, resulting in plants that are more than two metres tall with very large flowers, which in the case of *Dendrobium* 'Caesar Stripe', a cross with *Dendrobium stratiotes*, can be up to nine centimetres long. Hybridising these orchids has produced flowers of all sorts of colours. There are pink, white, red, yellow, green, orange, purple, violet, brown, burgundy and blue flowers and the big advantage is that they remain in good condition for a number of months. In addition, the flowers have a wonderful form.

Dendrobium spectabile has fantastic, strange flowers that seem to be misshapen because of the extent to which all the parts are twisted. These flowers grow up to eight centimetres long and have a honey scent. This species originates from New Guinea, the Solomon Islands and the island of Vanuatu, where they grow in trees in scorchingly hot swamp areas. The plant is called the Octopus Orchid though this name is also used for *Encyclia cochleata,* a totally different species found in tropical America.

The genus *Dendrobium* includes a large number of species with vivid yellow flowers. The golden-yellow flowers of *Dendrobium harveyanum* have long hairy petals surrounded by a beautifully fringed lip. It gives off a pleasant, sweet scent and is also pollinated by bees. The scent is a complex mixture of honey, primulas, cloves and mimosas. The flowers often have nectar tracks to guide the bees to the plant parts with nectar, like lines pointing to a target. These lines or marks are not always visible to the human eye since part of them lies in the UV spectrum. Bees can see them however, so flowers that appear evenly yellow to us display clear patterns to the bees.

Dendrobium *'Caesar Stripe'* has been bred by crossing the Antelope Orchid, >
Dendrobium stratiotes, with the popular **D. phalaenopsis.**

A gross deception

Ophrys is a genus of orchid with approximately 140 species found in Europe, North Africa and Asia Minor, principally in the region around the Mediterranean Sea. The flowers of these species all resemble various insects. Examples are the Bee Orchid (*Ophrys apifera*), the Fly Orchid (*Ophrys insectifera*) and the Bumblebee Orchid (*Ophrys fuciflora*). This resemblance is not accidental, as it is part of a subtle mechanism to provide for pollination. The flowers mimic female insects, so that males are attracted and land on the lip of the flower. It is the lip of the orchid that looks like an insect, as it is dark-coloured and is in certain places hairy, just like the females. There are also structures that are reminiscent of eyes. In the Fly Orchid the lip is black and shaped like an insect; the two petals are likewise black, long, narrow and pointed upward, so that they exactly resemble the antennae of an insect. In the Bee Orchid and many other species the lip is dark brown with a specific pattern of stripes and/or spots, and the lip's extremity is curved and velvety-haired like the abdomen of a bee or bumblebee. When the males try to mate with the flowers (this is called pseudocopulation), they get the pollen clumps or pollinia stuck to their body. When they then try to mate with a subsequent flower they bring the pollen that they carry to this flower, and so pollination is carried out. The imitation of sexual partners to lure pollinators is called 'sexual mimicry'. Almost every species of *Ophrys* is visited by a different insect species. The insects that let themselves be fooled are species from two genera of wasps (the dagger wasps *Trielis* and digger wasps *Gorytes*), and two genera of bees, *Eucera* or Longhorn Bees and *Andrena* or Sand Bees. The males position themselves with their heads toward the middle of the flower, so that the pollen is stuck there. *Andrena* bees approach the orchid differently and get pollen stuck to their abdomens.

Sex is also strongly driven in insects by their sense of smell. Females attract males by secreting sex pheromones. These substances differ depending on the species, and males can sometimes smell females of their species from a great distance. Male butterflies and moths can detect a female even at a distance of ten kilometres! *Ophrys* flowers have evolved to secrete the same scent substances as the sex pheromones from female insects. This means that every orchid species produces precisely the substance used by its pollinators as a pheromone! In fact the story is somewhat more complex, as an *Ophrys* flower produces a scent spectrum of more than a hundred different scent substances, some of which lure the male insects. There are in addition individual differences in this scent spectrum between flowers from different plants that occur in each other's vicinity. It is useful that each flower does not have exactly the same scent, because after a time the insects do realise that the flowers they visited were not 'the real thing'. Therefore they will avoid flowers with the same scents, but continue to visit flowers that smell somewhat differently. It may seem strange to us that the male insects can be so easily deceived by imitation females. However, in these species of bees and wasps the males hatch earlier in the springtime than the females, so that in the beginning there is a shortage of females. This period can last for two weeks. Most *Ophrys* species bloom just at that point in time when there are still no female insects available. The male insects are still young and inexperienced, and therefore let themselves be led up the garden path.

Pseudocopulation is also known to occur in other orchids, among them some Australian species (see below),

As its name suggests, the fly orchid, **Ophrys insectifera**, has flowers that resemble flies.

and several tropical species. *Trichoceros antennifera* is a South American species called 'la Mosca', the fly. It is a dark hairy flower that attracts male flies of a certain species. Also from South America is the *Trigonidium obtusum,* with remarkable triangular flowers that are pollinated by pseudo-copulation with bees of the genus *Trigona.* Recently it was also demonstrated that *Lepanthes glicensteinii* is pollinated by the fly *Bradysia floribunda,* belonging to the family of the Sciaridae, the family of moss flies or humus flies. Males of this fly species 'mate' with the flowers, even releasing sperm. It is supposed that this method of pollination could occur in numerous species of the genus *Lepanthes,* given that the flower structure within this genus shows little variation. *Lepanthes* is a genus of more than eight hundred species with mostly small flowers. Within this genus little gems can be found, such as *Lepanthes calodictyon,* that has splendidly marked leaves contrasting with bright red flowers.

It is conjectured that several orchid species are pollinated by pseudocopulation, without this having been actually observed. This is the case with the Asian genera *Haraella* and *Luisia. Luisia* is a genus of forty species of *Vanda*-like plants with small flowers that form on short flower stalks in the joints between leaves. The shapes of the flowers are rather bizarre and in some species the lip looks rather like that of the above-mentioned *Ophrys* species; they are thus also called Bee Orchids. *Haraella* is a genus with only one species, *Haraella odorata* from Taiwan. This is a miniature orchid with leaves that reach a maximum of seven centimetres long and flowers up to two centimetres in length. They are yellow and have a lip with a central glossy dark brown to violet marking, with fringes on the extremity. The brown marking shows up strongly against the yellow background of the remaining parts of the flowers, and this mimics a beetle. The plant is popular with aficionados because the flowers of this compact species give off a strong, sweet scent, reminiscent of lemon as well as mint.

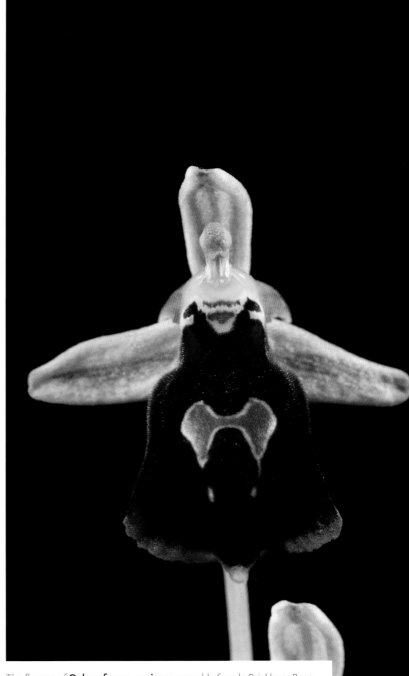

The flowers of **Ophrys ferrum-equinum** resemble female Bricklayer Bees **(genus Megachile or Chalicodoma).** The species name means 'horseshoe' due to the shining horseshoe-like spot on its lip.

< **Ophrys fuciflora** is a European species with a distribution from Southern Britain to Romania.
They are pollinated by Longhorn Bees and hoverflies which attempt to copulate with the flower.

Orchids
down under

The natural hybrid **Thelymitra crinita x macrophylla** has stunning blue flowers.

The strangest Australian orchids are perhaps the underground orchids of the genus *Rhizanthella*. These include *Rhizanthella gardneri* and *R. slateri*, which grow almost completely underground, with only the flowers emerging just above ground level. These are species that contain no chlorophyll, and live in symbiosis with soil fungi. They have no leaves and no roots, and consist only of pale elongated tubers that grow about ten centimetres under the ground. The scented, small flowers emerge just at soil level, but remain well hidden under the layer of fallen leaves. They are grouped in a sort of flower head that becomes up to five centimetres across and contains up to a hundred flowers. Pollination is carried out by all sorts of insects, such as small flies or termites. Fertilised flowers form a fleshy fruit that looks like a berry, in which between 20 and 150 seeds are present. It is thought that the berries are eaten by small marsupials who spread the seeds. *Rhizanthella* were only discovered in 1928, and have been only rarely observed. This is partly because they lead a hidden life, but also because they are rare and threatened. They thrive only under *Melaleuca uncinata* bushes, and cannot survive in ploughed farmlands.

A number of Australian orchids have bizarre-looking flowers. This occurs because they, like the European *Ophrys* species, are dependent for their pollination on male insects, which they try to lure into mating with them (pseudocopulation). This type of deception is estimated to occur in somewhere between a hundred to three hundred Australian species from nine genera. Most of their flowers have inconspicuous colours, often green, brown and red, and to humans they are odourless. Depending on the species, different male wasps are attracted, and in certain orchids, ants or leaf wasps are involved. Every orchid species is for the most part only pollinated by one specific insect species.

Australia is known for its unique fauna, with strange animal species such as kangaroos and platypuses. Its flora is just as unique; 85% of Australian flora is found nowhere else in the world. Orchids are well represented in Australia, with approximately eight hundred species in total. A quarter of these are tree-dwelling (epiphytic) species that only occur in the humid tropical belt along the North and East coasts. The remaining three-quarters of Australian orchids are terrestrial, and within this group quite a few bizarre flowers occur. There are species that lose their leaves during the dry period and survive thanks to underground tubers. Some species can even thrive in desert regions.

In a number of cases the flowers, or parts thereof, look strikingly like female insects, but a visual likeness is not really necessary; the most important factor appears to be scent. Sometimes the scent of the flowers alone is sufficient to drive the males wild. Some Australian orchid flowers produce precisely the same substances as the sex pheromones of a particular insect species, so that the males think they are dealing with females of their species. Research has shown that the bird orchid *Chiloglottis trapeziformis* secretes one specific chemical that only attracts the male wasps of *Neozeleboria cryptoides*. As an experiment this substance was synthetically manufactured and applied to pin heads. This was sufficient to attract the male wasps; in a number of cases

Pollinating wasp on **Caladenia bryceana**.

The flowers of **Pterostylis scabra**, the Green-veined Shell Orchid, form a trap for their pollinators, small humus flies.

the wasps even tried to mate with these pins! Orchids of the genus *Cryptostylis* also attract male wasps that sometimes choose the flowers over the 'real thing'! The wasps become so strongly attracted that there is a complete mating.

Another Australian group of wasp-pollinated orchids that imitates insects is *Caladenia*. This genus contains more than 150 species that are almost exclusively found in this country. They are terrestrial species that occur in scrubland and forests. Some species are gravely threatened or even extinct. Most Caladenias have very gracefully shaped flowers with long tails, which has earned them the name Spider Orchid, a name also given to the South American *Brassias*. One of the species with large flowers is *C. excelsa*, the flowers of which are thirty centimetres in diameter with long tail-like appendages. Another spectacular species is *C. huegelii*, with large green, red-striped flowers and a fringed lip. Unfortunately only several hundred examples of this species exist in nature.

Many Australian orchids have odd flowers, such as those of the Duck Orchid *Paracalaena nigrita*, the Rabbit Orchid *Leptoceras menziesii*, and the Hare Orchid *Leporella fimbriata* that is pollinated by male ants. The Hammer Orchid, *Drakaea glyptodon*, however beats them all. The flowers have a black glossy lip that on the extremity becomes a horizontal stalk, the middle of which has a hinged section,

so that the lip can tilt upwards against the column. The lip forms an imitation of the female of a certain species of wasp (*Zapilothynnus trilobatus*). These females are wingless and live underground. When they are sexually mature, they crawl above ground on a stem, in search of a partner. There they secrete a sex pheromone to attract the males. When a male notices a female, he lifts her up and they begin a lengthy mating session in the air. In the meantime he looks for nectar in flowers and passes this to her as a gift. After several meals, when she is satisfied, he deposits her back on the ground. Then she burrows herself back underground to look for a caterpillar, which she first paralyses, and onto which she lays an egg. The subsequent larvae feed on the paralysed caterpillar.

The flowers of the Hammer Orchid look fairly similar to these female wasps, but in particular they secrete exactly the same chemical substance. This is a molecule with a complex structure, only secreted by the females of this wasp species and the flowers of this type of orchid. The male wasps are fooled by the flowers, and land on the hairy lip of the flower. They rub their abdomens against it and still believe they are dealing with a suitable partner. Enraptured, they want to lift up their wingless lover to carry out a mating flight. Unfortunately, due to the hinged section in the centre of the flower they land violently against the column

The Dwarf Spider Orchid, **Caladenia caesarea**, grows in heathlands along the coast of Southwest Australia. Unfortunately, these areas are also populated by tourists who endanger their habitats.

The Underground Orchid **Rhizanthella gardneri**.

of the orchid, where they hit their head several times. Only then can the overwhelmed insect free itself and fly away. A variation of this mechanism is found again in the Elbow Orchid *Spiculaea ciliata*, with the added detail that the column contains hook-shaped structures on either side. When the insect rubs against the column, these hooks wrap themselves perfectly around its body, so that it remains hanging by its wings for several seconds. It must wrestle itself free, and in so doing pollination is achieved.

Yet more strange flowers are found in the genus *Pterostylis*, which contains about 120 Australian species. The topmost petals are fused together and form a sort of chamber, the lowest part of which can be closed off by the tilting of the lip. All the species have a lip that is sensitive to touch, and they are pollinated by small humus flies. The flies are attracted by the flowers because these look like certain mushrooms. The moment they touch the lip on the sensitive spot, the lip tilts so that they become caught in the flower. The weight of the flies amounts to only one milligram, but is sufficient to set this mechanism in action. The flies can then get out only if they follow a tunnel, which naturally leads them along a place where pollinia attach to their bodies.

Australian terrestrial orchids not only include bizarre monstrosities, but also a number of brilliantly coloured species. Intensely blue flowers, especially, are unique in the orchid world. There are several species of blue orchids that occur outside Australia, such as *Acacallis cyanea* from the Amazon region, but their colour cannot rival that of their Australian counterparts. The Sun Orchids (genus *Thelymitra*) in particular are famous for their sky-blue flowers. These are orchids whose blooms only open in sun and temperatures above 15°C, and close at evening or in insufficient light and heat. Within *Thelymitra* fifty or so species occur, half of which grow in Australia and the other half in areas ranging from New Zealand to the Philippines. While there are several blue-coloured species, such as *Thelymitra crinita* and *T. nuda*, there are also differently-coloured species, for example yellow and brown, or violet with orange or yellow, such as the splendid *Thelymitra variegata*. An exceptional feature of *Thelymitra* is that in contrast to other orchids, the flower lip has the same shape and colour as the other petals. By doing so they mimic flowers of the lily family, in order to entice pollinators without offering nectar or pollen in return. In some blue-flowered species the flowers have yellow pearl-shaped hairs in their centre. This is thought to be an imitation of pollen grains, to make the visiting insects believe that they will find pollen in these flowers. To make the imitation still better, the flowers also diffuse a scent, for example of lemon, while *T. stellata* even smells of cinnamon.

Transsexuals and drunken bees (Catasetinae and Stanhopeinae)

About three quarters of all flowering plants have bisexual (hermaphroditic) flowers, which means that they possess male organs that produce pollen as well as female organs with egg cells that develop into seeds after pollination. Some species, however, have unisexual flowers with one gender — these are known as dioecious plants. Only around 5% of flowering plants are dioecious, differing greatly from the animal kingdom where individuals are normally unisexual. A well-known example of a dioecious plant is the holly, where some trees have only female flowers and the others only male flowers. Female holly plants cannot form pollen, but bear berries after pollination from a male plant in the area. There is yet a third category that occurs, the monoecious plants. These have unisexual flowers, but they also have both male and female flowers on the same plant. An example is the hazel tree, the male catkins of which are very conspicuous in the late winter, while the small but bright purple female flowers bloom later and are much more discrete.

Within the orchid family most flowers are bisexual, but there is one group with unisexual flowers. These are primarily species within the genus *Catasetum*. This is an American genus with a hundred species that all produce bizarrely-shaped flowers. The male and female flowers differ for the most part so markedly that it was previously thought that the plants with male flowers belonged to a different species than those with female flowers. Some species have either male or female flowers, such as *Catasetum barbatum* and *C. deltoideum*. The environment of the plant influences which gender the flowers will have. Female flowers are twenty-five times more rare than the male, and are only formed by plants that get a great deal of light or nutrients. In other species both unisexual and bisexual flowers occur on the same plant. The bisexual flowers are however not functional, which means that they form no pollen and cannot be fertilised. In *Catasetum macrocarpum* female as well as bisexual flowers occur, and in *Catasetum cristatum, C. discolor, C. longifolium,* and *C. pileatum,* male as well as bisexual flowers are present.

The male flowers of *Catasetum* have thread-like appendages that grow to several centimetres long. When these are touched, the pollinia are violently hurled off onto the back of the pollinating insects. The pollinators are male Euglossine bees who do not live in social colonies like honeybees, but in nests with several females. The males lead a solitary and wandering existence and live for at least six months, which is exceptionally long for male bees. Approximately two hundred species of Euglossine bees exist, all found in Central and South America. In most species the males are handsomely metallic-coloured, either green, blue or gold. The males are drawn by the special scent of the orchids. The species *Catasetum expansum* for example smells of floor cleaner early in the day, but later in the day of dill seed and rye bread. During their visit to the flowers, bees scratch on the inside of the lip, releasing a scented liquid. They collect this liquid and carry it away in hollow sections in their hind legs, to use later to attract females. They become groggy from the sweet, musky scent, lose control over their movements and become clumsy and slow. But they turn over and over again back to another flower looking for the same experience, as if they cannot get enough. Because of their movements in the lip of the male flowers, the pollinia stick to them. In *Catasetum fimbriatum* the pollinia are fired off with a speed of up to twelve

Stanhopea radiosa has flowers that smell of cinnamon. They are found > in the wild on trees and rocky slopes along the west coast of Mexico.

kilometres per hour. This cannot be a pleasant experience, as a bee that has gone through this avoids all other male flowers from then on. Fortunately the female flowers look completely different, and are visited repeatedly.

Stanhopea is a genus of approximately 45 species from tropical regions of the Americas, in which the striking flowers hang down at the bottom of the plant; these plants therefore have the English name of 'Upside-down Orchids'. They are for the most part very large (up to 20 centimetres in size), waxy flowers with a bizarre shape, and commonly have a strong, intoxicating scent. A number of species are vanilla scented, but there are also species with fragrances that resemble those of medicines or spices. A very beautiful species from Mexico is Stanhopea tigrina; according to tradition these were cultivated by the Aztec Emperor Montezuma.

The flowers of Stanhopeas smell strongest early in the day, exactly when their pollinators are present. These are once more the male Euglossine bees. The flowers supply them with a scented substance with which they can then lure their female counterparts. The flower thus acts as a kind of 'perfume shop' for sex pheromones. In exchange for this pheromone, the flowers are pollinated. Bees approach the flowers from the side to collect the perfume from a cushion-like structure on the lip; this is where the scent substances are secreted. But because the lip is covered with an oily substance they slip and fall below; en route they are guided by two arms or horn-like projections of the lip, so that they touch precisely the top of the column and thus get pollinia attached to them. Each time they can only collect a very small quantity of scent substance, and are therefore obliged to risk several attempts, increasing the probability of pollination.

The flowers in this genus are generally short-lived, remaining for only two to five days, in contrast to many orchids whose flowers remain open for weeks or even months. This is perhaps also an adaptation to ensure that bees visit the flowers of other plants, because they have not yet collected enough perfume. This would increase the chances of pollination for the plant.

A comparable pollination mechanism is also found in species of the genus Gongora. Here, however, the bees hang upside down to reach the scent substance. They scratch

The flower of **Lycaste aromatica** smells like cinnamon and lemon.

the base of the flower's lip and are then numbed by these substances. In some species pollinia becomes attached to them in the process, as in Gongora truncata. In other species such as Gongora maculata the column is several centimetres long and curved, and is bent under the lip. When an insect lets go of the lip it lands on the column and slides completely along it. At the bottom of the column the bee is coated in pollen in a fraction of a second.

Coryanthes is another American genus with strangely shaped flowers. This name means literally 'helmet flower', but in English they are also known as Bucket Orchids. This name is very applicable, as will become apparent. The flowers are constructed so that they form a trap for their pollinating bees of the genera Euglossa and Eulaema. As in Stanhopea, the flowers hang down and the lip is transformed into a complicated structure: the scent substances are secreted in a helmet- or dome-shaped fixture at

< During pollination of **Gongora maculata,** bees glide over a long curved column.

Catasetum tenebrosum is a remarkable species from Peru and Ecuador with dark brown flowers and a yellow lip. The name *tenebrosum* means dark and refers to the colour of the petals.

the top connected via a tube to a bucket-like structure at the bottom. On the base of the lip there are two glands that secrete a liquid with which the bucket slowly becomes filled. The male bees are lured by the scent substance and try to collect this in flight from beneath the helmet. It is however a slippery business, and often they lose their grip and bump against the continually dripping glands. As soon as a drop touches their wings, they fall in the liquid-filled bucket. The only exit from this trap is along the top of the lip, via a narrow passage through which they must crawl. To get through this tunnel the soaked insects must climb onto a step, making contact with the stigma and pollen of the flower. The pollinia are stuck on their back like a rucksack so that they transfer them to the next flower. Before they get out of the flower they must however struggle for up to three-quarters of an hour. Having completely lost their bearings, the poor insects must first recover and dry out before they fly further. After a day or two, however, they let themselves be tempt-

ed again to go collect perfume in another flower, and with some good luck for the flower, or bad luck for the bee, he falls back into the bucket. He recognises in the meantime the way to the exit, and wriggles into the tunnel, where the meanwhile slightly shrunken pollinia remain hanging on the stigma and take care of fertilisation. Although he is roughly treated by the orchid, he is rewarded with the valuable perfume he needs to attract females. This takes place through a mating dance with complicated flight patterns and much buzzing, and meanwhile he diffuses the orchid perfume that makes him completely irresistible...

Euglossine bees also pollinate less strangely shaped orchids, for example, species from *Zygopetalum*. Most of the fifteen or so species have large, deliciously scented flowers that display surprising colour combinations from purple to brown, green and white. Their scent resembles that of hyacinths, daffodils or carnations. Zygopetalums are terrestrial South American orchids, most of which are of Brazilian origin. They must be cultivated in cool conditions to be able to bloom. In the past few decades Zygopetalums have become more and more popular and quite a number of hybrids have been produced.

The genus *Lycaste* likewise contains South American species with pleasant-smelling flowers also pollinated by Euglossine bees, this time both males and females. The flowers of *Lycaste aromatica* smell of cinnamon and lemon, *Lycaste locusta* and *L. brevispatha* of apple, *Lycaste deppei* of mint and eucalyptus, *Lycaste candida* of plums, and the flowers of *L. cochleata* smell of mango and apricot in the mornings and ginger in the evenings. Still other species smell respectively of green beans, oranges and pine resin.

Coryanthes senghasiana is a species from Peru, >
Colombia and Venezuela, that was first described in 1988.

Dracula and other horror stories

Dracula chimaera was named after a fire-breathing female monster from Greek mythology.

Orchids which are pollinated by flies usually have the most bizarre flowers of all. They are hairy with unobtrusive colours, usually brown and dark shades, or with dark markings, which particularly attract flies. The flowers usually have long tail attachments, with or without scent glands. They usually emit unpleasant odours, at least to humans, because these are smells that flies are attracted to. Moreover, the majority of these flowers set a trap for flies, who only get free after having fulfilled the purpose of pollination.

The genus *Dracula* contains more than one hundred species, all originating from Central America and the Northwest of the Andes; more than half of them grow in Ecuador. These plants prosper in shady and cool, misty climates. They derive their name from the notorious Count of Dracula, the blood drinking monster from the horror novel of the same name, written in 1897 by Bram Stoker. The vampiric Count Dracula has subsequently influenced the human imagination and was the inspiration for numerous films. The fact that orchids of this genus have been named after this vampire is probably due to their strange forms and dark colours. They have triangular flowers with a mobile lip and three long, spraddled slips. *Dracula vampira* possesses fascinating flowers that are dark or purple-striped with dark, long slips up to eleven centimetres long. In the wild this species grows only on trees at around 2000m elevation in two provinces of Ecuador. The form depicted here is named 'Night Angel'. The black markings of this species make the flower appear quite sinister. Black orchids are, like other black flowers, very precious to amateurs and collectors.

The flowers of **Porroglossum muscosum** catch flies by folding up their lip. >

Dracula vampira *'Night Angel'* has fascinating
flowers with slips up to eleven centimetres long.

Several orchids have black markings, but fully black flowers are rare. An example of an almost black flower is *Paphiopedilum* 'Black Velvet' or 'Candor Neat', a crossing of slipperworts. Another very dark cultivar is *Paphiopedilum* 'Starship Voodoo Magic'. However, wild species can also produce almost black flowers, for example *Maxillaria schunkeana*. This has dark-red to almost perfect black blooms.

The name "*Dracula vampira*" proves that botanists can have a feeling for drama. Another beautiful name is *Dracula vladtepes*. As those familiar with the story will know, the story of Dracula takes place for a large part in his castle in Transylvania, a region in Romania. Some claim that the author of the book got his inspiration from the notorious Vlad III, a fifteenth century ruler from Wallachia, in southern Romania. He was better known as Vlad Tepes, which translates as Vlad the Pikeholder. He was rumoured to have killed 100,000 people by spiking them with a sharp pole. Meanwhile the name Dracula originates from the Order of the Dragon, a secret order of knights who wanted to protect Christianity against the Ottomans. The father of Vlad Tepes, Vlad II, belonged to this order and was sometimes known as Vlad Drac, meaning Vlad the Dragon. The suffix '–ulea' means 'son of', so that Dracula means 'son of the dragon'.

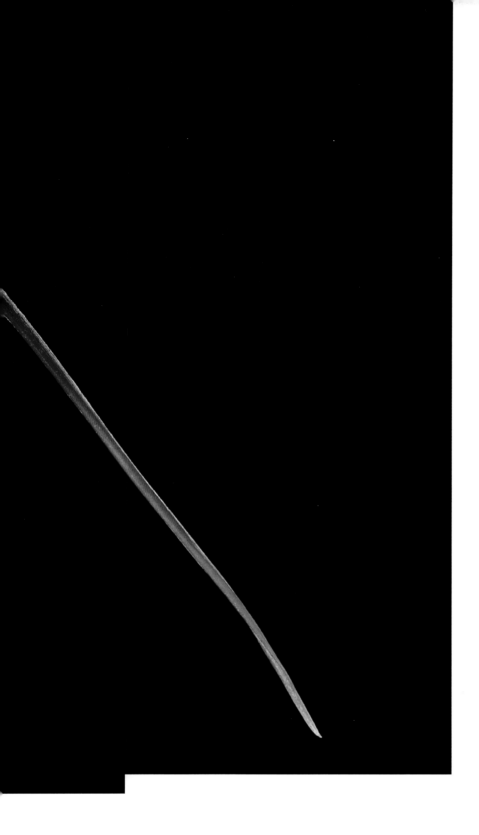

Vlad Tepes would therefore become Vlad Dracula. But because drac also means devil, Dracula can also be translated as 'son of the devil'. The plant name *Dracula vladtepes* is a direct referral to this story.

Within this genus other imaginative names were given, such as *Dracula cutis-bufonis*, which literally translates as the 'toad skin' orchid, and *Dracula diabola*, the devil(ish) orchid. Some *Dracula* species are reminiscent of blood-sucking monsters because their flowers are long and thickly haired, emulating bats. This is the case with *D. polyphemus*, the Cyclops Orchid. This species was named after Cyclops,

the one-eyed monster of Greek mythology. Cyclops held Odysseus prisoner in a cave and ate several of his companions. This species possesses pretty red, densely hairy flowers with a neat white lip. Even more densely haired is *Dracula chimaera*, with cream-coloured brown speckled flowers and brown red tails. It is called after the chimaera, another figure from Greek mythology. This was a fire-spitting female monster with multiple heads; her body was composed of parts of dragon, snake, goat and lion. In the medieval Christian art she was a symbol for satanic forces. The bizarre smell of *Dracula chimaera* contains components reminiscent of yeast, algae, mushrooms, and even cocoa.

Both the above-mentioned species disperse an odour similar to mushrooms. Research has shown that they are pollinated by particular flies that prefer to lay their eggs in mushrooms, so their larvae can feed on them. The white lip of the flower imitates the mushroom. Because the flower disperses the same odour as the mushrooms, the flies are misled and lay their eggs there. In the meantime they get pollen clods glued to them, which they take with them to another flower, and thereby take care of pollination. The larvae which come out of the eggs, however, will not lead a long life, since they can not feed themselves with flower tissue and therefore they starve.

The fly-pollinated genus *Zootrophion* contains many bizarre flowers. The name "Zootrophion" means zoo and the name was adopted because the flowers in this group are said to resemble the heads of many types of animals, quite often those of birds. There are about twelve species found from Central America to the Andean mountains. In all species the petalsare fused, so that a closed flower is created. Two openings or slits on the sides of the flower resemble eyes. *Zootrophion griffin* was named after the griffin, a mythological animal with the head of an eagle and the body of a lion. The strange flowers of these orchids and their function have long attracted the attention of researchers. Most of these flowers are brown, and some are hairy on the outside, which attracts flies to crawl inside and lay their eggs. Darwin found insect eggs in the flowers of this species (this is known as brood-site mimicry). The mechanism is similar to that of some Asclepiadaceae (milkweed family), such as *Ceropegia* species, which also attracts flies.

Porroglossum muscosum has transparent pale yellow to salmon-coloured flowers with three long tails, reminiscent of the flowers of *Masdevallia*. It is a species from the Andes, stretching from Venezuela to Ecuador, where it is found in cloud forests at a height of between 1600 and 3000 meters. Their flowers are displayed on a strikingly hairy stalk, from which the species obtains its scientific name 'muscosus', meaning 'mossy'. The flower also has an extraordinary moving lip which can take two positions. The normal position during the day is downwards, but when the lip is touched, it immediately pops upwards. Every insect touching the flower is kept prisoner in this way against the generative organs of the flower. Pollen clumps become glued to it and in the meantime it rubs any pollen that it might have brought from somewhere else onto the

Zootrophion lappaceum (Cryptophoranthus endresianus)
originates from Colombia.

pistil of the flower. After half an hour the lip pops back into its original position and the insect can fly away. The lip closes itself at night and opens again in the morning. The genus *Porroglossum* consists of thirty species, all of which have a similar mobile lip.

Dracula chimaera >
p. 116-117: **Dracula polyphemus,** the Dracula orchid, has flowers with many hair-like protrusions and they smell like mushrooms.

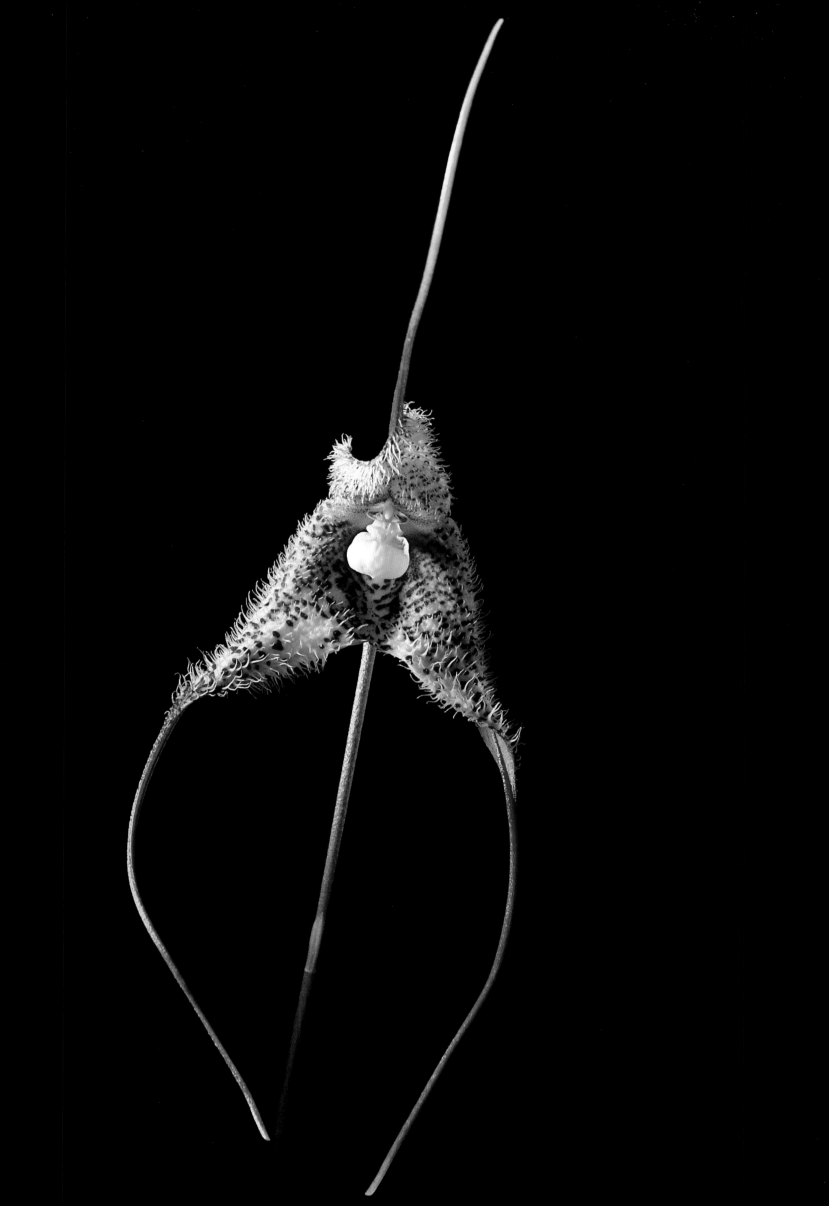

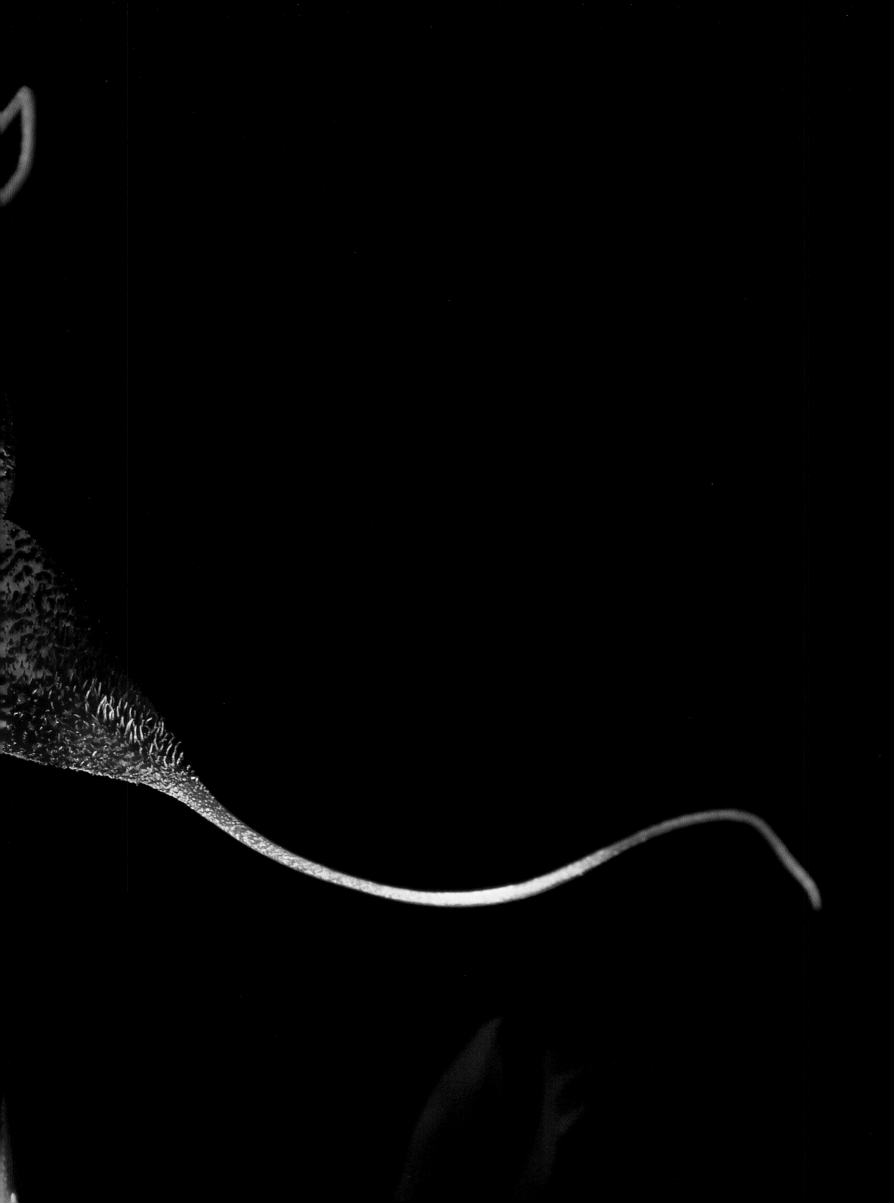

Slipper orchids and slippery customers

The so-called 'Slipper Orchids' with their sac-shaped lips (saccate) are among the most eye-catching of all orchids. The vast majority originate beyond Europe, and only one species is found in Western Europe, the Lady's Slipper Orchid or Slipper Orchid (*Cypripedium calceolus*). This is an eye-catching plant with brown petals and a yellow slipper, growing in forests and meadows. Unfortunately, it has become very rare.

Worldwide, there are three main groups within the Slipper Orchids, each in different parts of the world. The first group is the genus *Cypripedium*, to which the Lady's Slipper Orchid belongs; it has about forty species, which grow in Asia, North America and Europe. They are all terrestrial orchids preferring regions with a temperate climate. *Cypripedium fasciolatum* grows in the south of China, in Sichuan province, and is one of the *Cypripedium* species with the largest flowers, together with *C. kentuckiense* from the USA. Compared to this, the flowers of *Cypripedium plectrochilum* are real dwarfs, growing no larger than three centimetres. This species grows wild from the north of Myanmar down to the south of China.

Cypripedium formosanum has beautiful white flowers that are dotted with red. What is special about this species is that the opening of the lip is on the front side and not at the top; the back of this opening is often yellow. This is clearly designed to attract insects that will aid pollination. Its second name comes from the former name for the island of Taiwan, Formosa.

The second group of Slipper Orchids consists of the Asian genus *Paphiopedilum*, a group of plants with large and rather special flowers. There are about sixty species that can be found from India to the jungles of Southeast Asia. Most grow on the ground or on rocks but some grow as epiphytes on trees; they can be found at an altitude of up to two thousand metres. They usually have a limited area of distribution, and for several species only a small number of habitats in nature are known. Paphiopedilums were named after Paphos, another name for Aphrodite or Venus, the goddess of love, and pedilon means slipper, hence the name Slipper Orchid. According to legend, Venus lost her slipper on the isle of Cyprus, when she was hunting with Adonis, her lover. The couple had had to take shelter because of a rainstorm and they had taken the opportunity to make love. After that, Venus failed to notice that she had lost her slipper. A shepherd woman found it, but when she tried to pick it up, the slipper immediately transformed into a beautiful slipper-shaped flower instead.

Paphiopedilums are pollinated by flies, and although most do not have obtrusively smelling flowers, some give off a faint urine-like odour, such as *P. villosum, P. insigne* and *P. barbatum*. One of the most spectacular species within the genus is *Paphiopedilum rothschildianum*. This attractive plant is named after the wealthy 19th century English politician, art collector and fervent orchid lover, Baron Ferdinand de Rothschild. He was a member of the influential von Rothschild dynasty of bankers, a family originally from Austria. His home was Waddesdon Manor in the English county of Buckinghamshire. This property was built in the style of a French castle and within its walls, he displayed his highly valuable collections of paintings, furniture, tapestries and ceramics. He was friends with Queen Victoria who often visited. In fact she saw electric lighting, a recent invention at the time, for the

Phragmipedium wallisii x longipetalum >

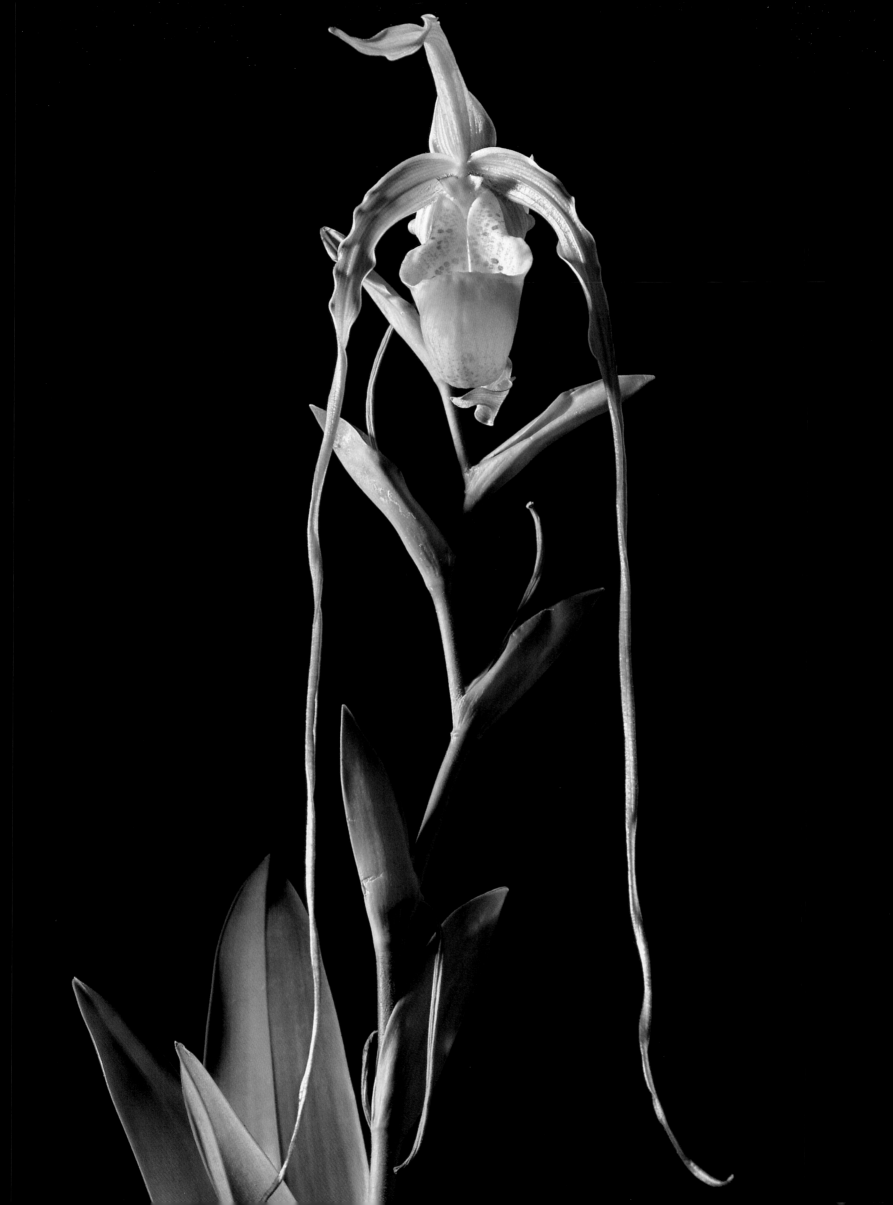

first time there. The de Rothschilds had glasshouses with wonderful collections of orchids and tropical plants in various domains across Europe, such as Frankfurt, Vienna, Ferrières (near Paris) and in Gunnersbury, London.

In 1867, *Paphiopedilum rothschildianum* was first sold in Europe by the British company F. Sander & Co. This orchid has the largest flowers of the genus and is often known as the 'King of the Paphs'. Flowering stems can reach up to one metre long, on which three to seven beautiful flowers develop, making the flowering stem up to 34 centimetres long. At the centre of each flower, as in other *Paphiopedilum*, are hair-like structures that attract pollinating flies.

These hairs mimic aphid colonies that lure parasitising Syrphid flies of the species *Dideopsis aegrota*. These flies are insects that mimic bees, but are smaller and have less stout bodies which are able to hover on a single spot. They are beneficial insects to gardeners as their larvae feed on large quantities of aphids while the adult flies aid pollination of various flowers. In nature, the female Syrphid flies lay their eggs among aphid colonies.

The hair-like structures on the flowers are located on a shield-shaped part of the bloom directly above the lip. The Syrphid flies are unable to make a firm landing and as a result they often fall into the slipper-shaped lip. Once inside they are unable to fly out of the slipper-shaped petal due to inward folds. In addition, the flies are unable to crawl out because the sides of the slipper are too smooth. Their only way out is via the sides, where hairs, one above another, form an escape ladder. This is no accident of course because it takes the fly past the the pollinia and stigma. In their escape pollen becomes adhered to their backs while pollen from other flowers rubs off on the stigma thus pollinating the bloom.

Paphiopedilum rothschildianum is not only one of the most beautiful species within the group, but also one of the rarest. It is found only on Borneo, in the area surrounding Mount Kinabalu, the highest mountain (4101m) of Southeast Asia. It has been found in four sites, on steep slopes and inaccessible cliffs at an altitude of 600 to 1200 metres. The Kinabalu region was once an isolated and difficult to access location. Today, it is a tourist attraction and visited by over two hundred thousand visitors per year. Many tourists are attracted by the orchids, and unfortunately a number of plants are stolen. Two of the four known habitats of this spe-

Paphiopedilum rothschildianum was named after the wealthy orchid lover Baron Ferdinand de Rothschild.

cies have already been destroyed and all are threatened by plundering from illegal orchid hunters despite the remaining plants being located inside the National Park. Mount Kinabalu is also home to many other rare and threatened orchids. In 1990, eighteen important orchid sites were discovered by researchers, however, three years later half of these were destroyed due to logging.

Another spectacular species is *Paphiopedilum sanderianum*. This almost legendary species is regarded as one of the most endangered orchids on earth, and highly sought after by collectors. The petals of these wonderfully veined flowers can reach a length of up to 90cm and droop in a graceful, wavy shape. One of Sander's plant collectors found this species in 1885 in the rainforest of Sarawak, a Malay province in Northwest Borneo. After that, it was not found again and was considered extinct. As a result, only a few cultivated plants were available on the market, sold at outrageously high prices. In 1978, this species was rediscovered, but the exact site where it grows is kept secret. Several attempts followed by orchid collectors and scientific institutes to obtain the species for research or for artificial

propagation. Eric Hansen's captivating account of his journey with two American orchid enthusiasts and two native guides to Borneo's Fire Mountain is a joy to read. He describes how they climbed steep slopes, making their way with difficulty through a wall of plants and razor-sharp rocks, pulling themselves up by grasping slippery roots and rock ledges as sharp as glass. During their dangerous journey one of the guides almost lost his life, but in the end they were rewarded by the fabulous sight of a mountain wall full of blooming plants of this orchid to photograph. Each team member paid close to three thousand five hundred dollars for the expedition. Hansen relates almost comically how astonished the native guides were when they discovered that the party had travelled almost twenty thousand kilometres, spent so much money and risked their lives just to witness these flowers in bloom.

Both species mentioned above have several, very large flowers on each stem. Consequently, they have been used as parents for multi-floral *Paphiopedilum* hybrids. More and more garden centres offer these. What is so nice about these plants is that they have multiple flowers on the same flower stem, one after the other, and thus blooming occurs over a long period of the year. They are easy houseplants, if you don't leave them without water for too long.

Most Paphiopedilums only form one or two flowers per stem and have flowers of more modest dimensions than the above-mentioned species, yet they still possess fairy-tale beauty. Species from the Parvisepalum section that originate mainly from southern China and Vietnam are very special. There are a number of white and pink types among them, e.g. *Paphiopedilum delenatii*, which has white flowers with a pink lip. These species were introduced into France at the beginning of the twentieth century. However, all the plants, died, except for one in the collection of the famous orchid grower Lecoufle near Paris. By self-pollination seedlings were produced and plants became available to hobby growers. The plant was seemingly lost in nature and feared extinct. In the nineties, however, this plant was rediscovered in Vietnam. This made it possible to mass propagate it in The Netherlands resulting in large numbers being available on the open market.

Until 1979, it was thought that there were no yellow Paphiopedilums. Then *Paphiopedilum armeniacum* was discovered with wonderful golden-yellow flowers. This species is only found on steep limestone cliffs in the southern Chinese province of Yunnan. The name "armeniacum" is Latin for 'apricot coloured' and does not mean that the plant has Armenian origin. According to the original Chinese description, the flowers of this species were supposed to be apricot coloured, but interestingly all flowers of cultivated specimens are yellow. It is uncertain why this discrepancy occurred, perhaps the first description was incorrect, or there are specimens with apricot flowers. If this is the case they have not been rediscovered but it is something orchid lovers secretly hope for.

The third group of slipper orchids consists of the South American genus *Phragmipedium*. There are about fifteen species, which naturally occur in humid places, e.g. near waterfalls and alongside river beds. Some species within this genus have very long petals, such as *P. giganteum*. Petals of this species grow as long as sixty centimetres. The record is perhaps set by *Phragmipedium caudatum* with petals up to seventy-five centimetres long. Soon after the buds open they are short but they continue to grow as the flower ages. They often have green or brown flowers. Like the *Paphiopedilum* the Slipper forms a trap for flies that can only escape by crawling along the pollinia, thus transporting pollen. The flowers of several species give off a faint urine-like odour, which helps lure flies. The function of the long petals remains unclear. However, since they often droop to the ground it has been suggested that they serve to let potential pollinators crawl up to the centre of the flower.

Within *Phragmipedium* there are species with brighter coloured flowers and shorter petals. This is the case of *Phragmipedium schlimii*, which has pink, sweet scented blooms. Likewise the beautiful *Phragmipedium besseae* is a species with bright orangey-red or sometimes yellow flowers. These are endemic to cloud forests along the eastern slopes of the Andes in Columbia, Ecuador and Peru. This species was first discovered in 1981 in Peru, and later also in Ecuador. Their discovery caused a sensation in the orchid world because no orange or red slipper orchids were previously known. As a result, these plants were sold at high prices and even small specimens with one or two shoots fetched $600. Various sites where the plants naturally occur were initially plundered, but fortunately within a few years plants were successfully propagated from seeds resulting in large quantities of inexpensive plants and reducing the threat to wild populations.

123

< **Cypripedium plectrochilum** is an Asian Venus Shoe with
small flowers of less than three centimetres.

The hybrid of **P. rothschildianum** and **P. sanderianum**
results in a plant with spectacular flowers.

In 2001, the orchid world was once again thrown into commotion by the discovery of a new species, *Phragmipedium kovachii* from the Amazon jungle of Peru. Orchid experts wrote that this was the most spectacular and the most sensational species to be discovered in a century. It has dark pink to purple flowers that can grow up to fifteen centimetres wide. The orchid was offered for sale alongside a road to an amateur American enthusiast who smuggled the plant out of the country. It not only caused excitement among growers and orchid lovers, but also among scientists who entered a race to be the first to officially describe it. In order to do so, a valid description of the plant has to appear in a scientific journal. The botanist Christenson forwarded a description of the species under the name *Phragmipedium peruvianum* to the journal of the American Orchid Society, but this appeared too late. Only fourteen days before that account was published, another description of this species calling it *P. kovachii* was written by staff of the Selby Gardens in their journal Selbyana. In order to be first, Selby Gardens published a special edition only featuring this orchid's description!

This was despite Christenson's account being written months before, but when it comes to naming plants, it is the publication date that counts.

Smaller genera, such as *Selenipedium* and *Mexipedium* are also Slipper Orchids. In Mexico *Mexipedium xerophyticum* there is a species with white to light pink flowers that closely resemble the Chinese Paphiopedilums. This species was first found in 1985 in the province of Oaxaca, but the exact site was kept secret so that the population would not be plundered. These plants grow on steep limestone cliffs and are part of a unique vegetation adapted to drought.

The magnificent **Cypripedium formosanum** originates from Taiwan. >

Tiny
jewels

The so-called Pleurothallidinae are a group of fly-pollinated orchids. This is a group of four thousand species from thirty genera of which most are miniature plants, including *Pleurothallis*. Because the flowers are proportionally small they were not grown much except by a few specialist amateur growers. *Pleurothallis* is probably the largest orchid genus, with more than eleven hundred species. It includes very diverse forms of often small plants with tiny flowers, which are often exceptionally beautiful at close range. It is only when they are held to the light that their full delicate and translucent nature is revealed. The flowers of *Pleurothallis schiedei* are remarkable; they have whitish appendages dangling like the fringes of a curtain. These move in the slightest breeze and stand out against the dark background of the flowers which attracts pollinating flies.

Most *Pleurothallis* grow in very humid rain and cloud forests in deep shade, where they can be found growing as epiphytes on small branches. Cloud forests are tropical mountain forests but at high altitudes, which are covered every day by banks of mist and fog. Many orchids grow in such habitats, in fact, forty-seven different species have been recorded on a single tree. Some species have large leaves, such as *P. cyanea*, that grow up to thirty centimetres in length.

The genus *Restrepia*, whose flowers have a characteristic form, also falls within the Pleurothallidinae group. It has relatively large flowers in comparison with its small scale. Like numerous 'fly flowers', they have tiny spots, which in certain species is replaced by stripes. The two lower sepals are united to form one large petal, which stands below and behind the lip. The upper central sepal is the shape of an antenna, and this one has a gland that secretes a scent that lures insects. Under a microscope the cells of this gland resemble minute mushrooms.

Pleurothallis truncata is a species from Ecuador with bright orange, round flowers that produce dozens of blooms at the same time.

Equally as strange are the flowers of the *Masdevallia* genus, most of which are pollinated by flies, but some also by birds. They have triangular flowers with long tail-like spurs, and sometimes unpleasant odours. *Lepanthes*, a related genus, discussed earlier, as well as the genus *Scaphosepalum*, that has some thirty species from Central and South America, which also grow in the humid coolness of cloud forests. All species have tail-like spurs, which appear, one after the other, at the end of the inflorescence.

Three percent of all orchids are thought to be pollinated by birds, such as **Masdevallia coccinea**. >

The flowers of **Restrepia antennifera 'Gigantea'** have
nectaries at the end of antenna-like sepals.

128

Talpinaria bivalvis is also known under the Latin name of **Pleurothallis talpinaria**. >

Rotting elephants
and mobiles

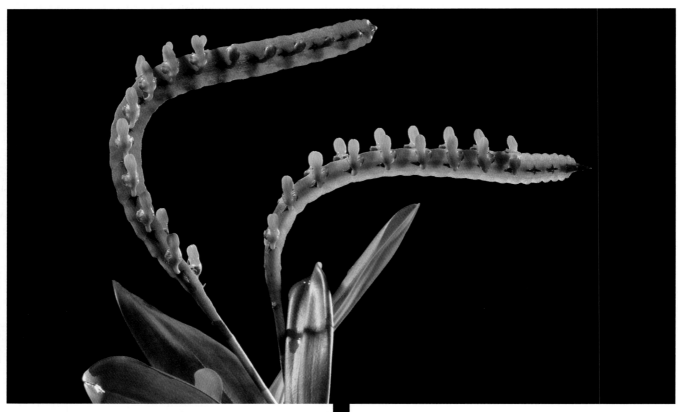

Bulbophyllum falcatum has a wide flattened flower stem, with small flowers positioned on both sides. Each flower is less than one centimetre and produces copious amounts of nectar that envelopes the entire flower.

Fly-pollinated flowers ordinarily give off unpleasant odours to our sense of smell. Among the orchids, species of the genus *Bulbophyllum* are especially foul smelling. This is one of the largest orchid genera consisting of an estimated thousand species. These include those species sometimes classified under the genus *Cirrhopetalum*. The majority originate from the tropics of Africa, but some come from South America. Their smell really gives away the fact that they are pollinated by flies! There are species with flowers that smell of dung or urine, others smell of blood, or worse, of bait and rotting flesh. *Bulbophyllum beccarii*, a species from the rainforest in the lowlands of Borneo, is named after the Italian botanist Odoardo Beccari. He spent three years exploring the primeval forest on Sarawak, where he collected and studied plants, insects and shells. He even discovered luminous mushrooms that emitted enough light to read a newspaper. He described the flowers of *Bulbophyllum beccarii* as stinking like a thousand dead elephants. This species has long rhizomes enabling plants to gradually manoeuvre themselves on tree trunks to maximise their access to light. The

This **Cirrhopetalum** has appendages and hairs that move with the   >
slightest breeze, thereby attracting flies that pollinate the flowers.

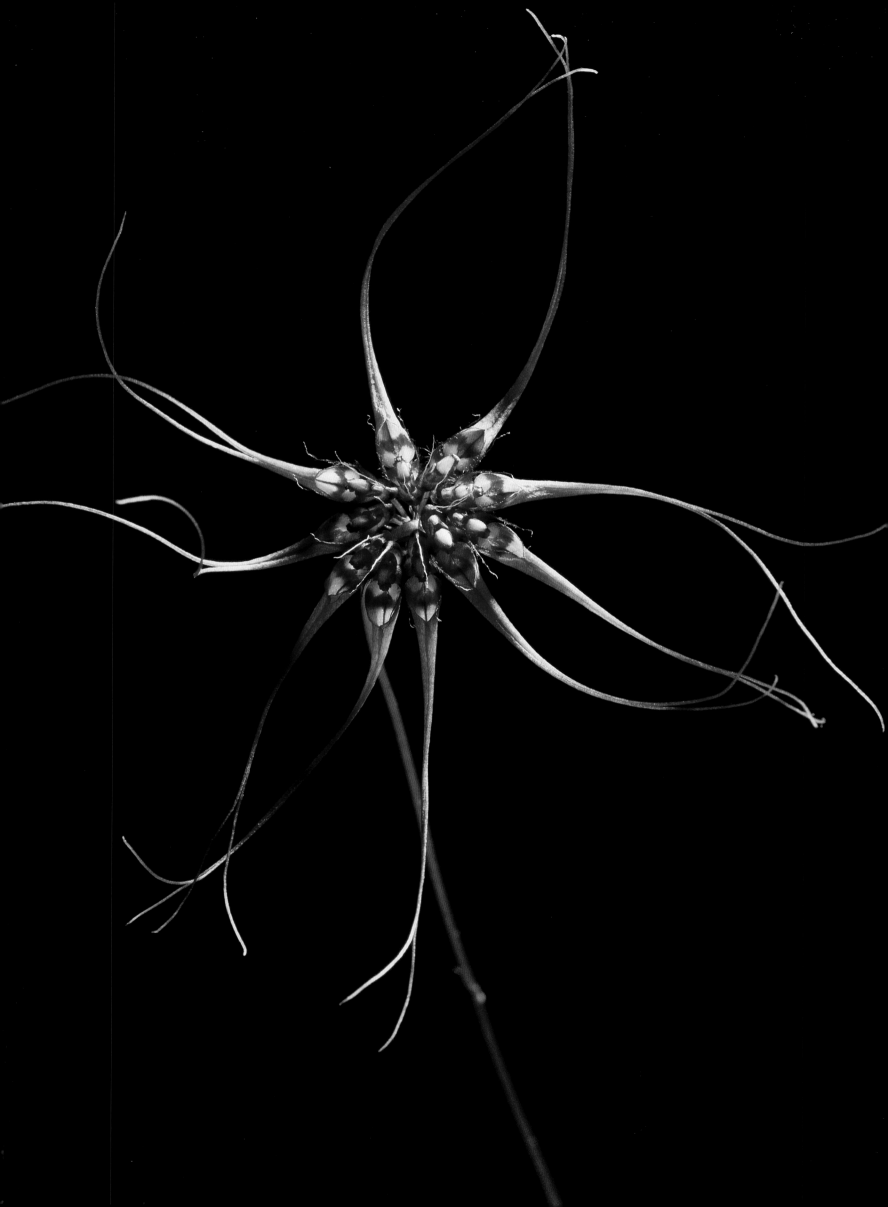

large flowers which emit a smell of dirty socks in the morning and rotting-fish in the afternoon!

Fortunately, not all Bulbophyllums smell bad: the beautiful flowers of *Bulbophyllum lobbii* have a very agreeable scent that is reminiscent of jasmine and orange blossom. *Bulbophyllum ambrosia* has small red-striped flowers whose scent, according to some, is close to bitter almonds; *Bulbophyllum cocoinum* has a scent reminiscent of dried coconut while *B. buntingii* gives off a sweet scent like freshly mown hay.

It is not only the scent, but also the construction of the flowers that is designed to accommodate pollination by flies. In contrast to bees, flies aren't very goal-oriented flyers. In their typical hyperactive way, flies move from side to side before landing. To exploit this, fly-pollinated orchids often have long protrusions or 'tails'. For example, *Bulbophyllum medusae* has numerous white flowers positioned together in a spherical shape with fine red speckled ribbons that grow up to fifteen centimetres long. This species was named after the Medusa, a mythological woman with snakes instead of hair. Long protruding flower parts often occur in *Cirrhopetalum*, a genus often included in *Bulbophyllum*. *Cirrhopetalum gracillimum* is a small species with fine red flowers and long tails, originating from Thailand, Myanmar, Malaysia and further east in Australia and the Solomon Islands. This species grows on tree trunks in the rainforest and the flowers give off a scent reminiscent of the sea, specifically of algae and crustaceans. Meanwhile, the flowers of *Cirrhopetalum gracillimum* have a purple-coloured 'eye' at the centre which dances in the slightest breeze. This appears to attract the attention of flies.

Both *Bulbophyllum* and *Cirrhopetalum* have a hinged lip allowing this flower part to move. Furthermore, numerous species have mobile appendages, for example small tufts of hair-like bristles that make the lip move up and down at the slightest breeze, such as in *Bulbophyllum barbigerum*. Other species have all kinds of fringes and ribbons, movable gills or even shapes that resemble miniature seats. The movable hairs of *B. phalaenopsis* mimic crawling maggots in rotting flesh!

Bulbophyllum grandiflorum has strange flowers
that can grow up to ten centimetres long.

plants have stiff, bowl-shaped leaves to catch humus and vegetable mould and pendulous inflorescences that consist of hundreds of red or yellow red-veined flowers. Another special species with respect to its smell and appearance is *B. rothschildianum*, a species from the north east of India with long leather-like leaves and eye-catching flowers.

Bulbophyllum phalaenopsis has thick, leathery leaves that grow to more than half a metre long with strange, hairy, purple flowers. This species occurs in the tropical humid lowlands of Papua New Guinea. The flowers stink badly, attracting flies that lay their larvae on the flowers and whilst doing so transfer pollen. Its English name 'corpse orchid' gives an indication of the stench the flowers emit. Closely related to this species is *Bulbophullum macrobulbon*, whose flowers are carrion scented. Other species have flowers with a fish smell, such as *Bulbophyllum singaporeanum* and *Bulbophyllum echinolabium*. The latter also has wonderful,

< **Bulbophyllum phalaenopsis** has huge flowers that smell
of decomposing meat to attract pollinating flies.

Butterflies *and* hummingbirds

Some orchids are pollinated by butterflies, yet others by moths. As discussed earlier, moths are attracted to white flowers that are night scented. In contrast, butterflies are irresistibly attracted to red, pink and yellow flowers. While some moths can hover a bit like a hummingbird, butterflies cannot. Butterflies are not elegant flyers, and flutter from flower to flower. Consequently, they need more space to land. Therefore, a horizontally stretched lip serves as a good landing site. Nectar is offered in long, narrow tube-shaped spurs that give off a pleasant, sweet scent. All butterflies possess a long proboscis enabling them to drink nectar. While feeding the pollinia is brushed by the insect and adheres to their proboscis.

The South African orchid *Disa uniflora* is pollinated by butterflies. The genus *Disa* contains about one hundred terrestrial species that occur in Africa, for the most part in southern Africa. Due to its large, wonderfully coloured flowers, *Disa uniflora* is the most popular species in cultivation. It is a magnificent species with flowers that are ordinarily red, but sometimes white, yellow or pink. They have a short spur, which contains nectar. Wonderful hybrids have been made of this species and others such as *Disa cardinalis, D. racemosa* and *D. tripetaloides*. These cultivated forms can be found in crimson, bright orange, pink or yellow. Unfortunately, these are not easy to grow. One difficulty of their cultivation is that the plants must be continuously kept in wet soil with low nutrients and grown where temperatures are not too high.

Pyramidal orchids, *Anacamptis pyramidalis*, are also butterfly pollinated. These have densely flowered inflorescences which are pale pink or very dark. This terrestrial species predominantly grows along the Mediterranean Sea but also in the dunes of Western Europe. It is also found in-

creasingly along road verges. An example from tropical Asia is the fire orchid, *Renanthera imschootiana*, which has wonderful orange-red flowers that remain fresh for months. This orchid grows in the wild as an epiphyte in Myanmar (Burma), in Vietnam and in Northwest India. The plants are branched and grow upwards (monopodial growth). Older specimens can achieve a height of several metres. Within this genus there are about fifteen other species, all with wonderfully coloured flowers.

There are also orchids that deceive butterflies, enticing them close enough to secure pollination but failing to produce a nectar reward. This is the case of the South American species *Epidendrum radicans*. The orange-red flowers of this species mimic the flowers of others that occur in the area. The mimicked flowers are *Asclepias curassavica* and *Lantana camara*, which produce copious amounts of nectar. The butterflies fail to notice the difference between the orchid and these flowers. Consequently, they visit orchids regularly transferring pollen as they go.

A species closely related to *Epidendrum radicans* is *Epidendrum ibaguense*. Both species have red flowers, but instead of being pollinated by butterflies, *E. ibaguense* is pollinated by birds, notably hummingbirds. Hummingbirds (family: Trochilidae) are small, mostly brightly coloured birds that live in the Americas. They are real acrobats, with the ability to hover in one place, move forwards, sideways and even backwards, a bit like a helicopter, but much nimbler and quicker. They can reach up to more than 60 wing beats per minute during which their heart rate reaches an incred-

Each inflorescence of **Epidendrum schomburgkii** resembles a firework. >

ible 1200 beats per minute. They feed on nectar, a sweet, nutrient-rich liquid that is produced in some flowers, but also eat insects, which form their main source of protein. To obtain nectar from flowers hummingbirds need to hover in front of the bloom and suck the sweet liquid with their long tongue. The Brazilian name of these magnificent little birds is 'Bejaflor', which means 'flower kisser'. Hummingbird pollinated flowers are generally red and tube-shaped, adapted specifically to the shape and curve of the birds' beak. Flowers of *Epidendrum schomburgkii* are this colour and shape. This species is sometimes regarded as a variety of *Epidendrum ibaguense*, which reaches more than two metres in height in its native range between Venezuela to Brazil. However, its flowers are almost twice the size of *E. ibaguense*.

All *Epidendrum* species originate from America. In the wild *Epidendrum ibaguense* and *E. radicans* can cover entire mountainsides and make them orange. In some areas they can escape from cultivation and proliferate in the wild as weeds. These species have bamboo-like stems and small, succulent leaves and racemes of brightly coloured pink or red flowers.

Initially, all tropical orchids were called *Epidendrum* by Linnaeus. This name means 'on a tree' and refers to the ability of numerous tropical orchids to grow on the branches of trees as epiphytes. As new orchid species were discovered the full realisation of how many epiphytic orchids exist became apparent. The large genus *Epidendrum* had species reclassified into other groups making it smaller. During the past few decades however, entire groups have been re-allocated to the genera *Encyclia* and *Prostechea*. Despite this it still contains around eight hundred species.

Another type of orchid visited by hummingbirds is *Stenorrhynchos speciosum*. This species grows on the ground or epiphytically in cloud forests in Ecuador, at an altitude of 2000 - 3000 metres. These plants have decorative leaves with silvery variegation that form a rosette.

According to scientists, three percent of all orchids are pollinated by birds. Several American orchids are pollinated by hummingbirds, such as *Comparettia's, Sophronitis* and *Cochlioda rosea* and all have brightly coloured flowers, such as orange, red or pink. Because birds, unlike butterflies, do not have a developed sense of smell, the flowers are odourless. Within the genus *Masdevallia* there are some

Stenorrhynchos speciosum grows in the cloud forests of Ecuador and is pollinated by hummingbirds.

species pollinated by hummingbirds, such as *Masdevallia coccinea*. This genus contains about 380 species that grow in rainforests, from southern Mexico to southern Brazil. Fifty species have, unfortunately, been placed on Red Lists as threatened species. The sepals of these flowers grow together to form a three cornered hat-like structure, often with long tails. The lip is usually very small and unsightly. Most species grow at high altitudes, where it is relatively cold. This is the case for almost all bird-pollinated orchids because at altitude it is too cold for most insects.

137

<   **Disa uniflora** grows along the streams on Table Mountain in South Africa.

The magnificently coloured flowers of the Fire Orchid
Renanthera imschootiana attract butterflies.

Maxillaria, notably *Maxillaria fulgens*, is another American genus which undergoes pollination by hummingbirds. Their flowers display very diverse colours. However other species are pollinated by bees or even wasps. These flowers produce oil or wax, which is collected by bees and probably used as material for nests. *Maxillaria nigrescens* has large dark-red flowers that give off a unique, bold perfume. It is an incomparable scent, reminiscent of violets and other fragrances. Since its flowers smell, this species is presumed pollinated by insects not birds.

Hummingbirds do not occur outside America, but there are birds that strongly resemble them, notably the 'sunbirds' (family: Nectariniidae). They occur in the tropical regions of Africa and Asia and glint like brightly coloured jewels. Just like hummingbirds, they can hover in front of flowers to drink nectar, but they are unable to fly backwards. Most species occur in forests, but a few live in deserts. Sunbirds are the chief pollinators of some Asian orchids such as *Dendrobium lawesii*. These orchids are brightly coloured and are tube-shaped and curved to allow the bird's bill to fit snugly. They are odourless and do not have wide openings as landing strips are not required. Such flowers have interesting pollinia that match the colour of the pollinating bird's beak, usually grey, in contrast to the yellow pollinia of most other orchids. The reason for this is because the pollinia must land on the beak unnoticed to avoid it being brushed off. A last characteristic is their thick petals, which avoids them becoming damaged when the bird feeds. Examples of such flowers are *Dendrobium lawesii, D. sophronitis, D. roseum* and *D. flammula*, all these originate from the highlands of New Guinea.

The red tubular flowers of **Dendrobium lawesii** are pollinated >
by Sunbirds, which resemble hummingbirds.

Glossary of terms

– **Botanical species**	plant occurring in the wild, in contrast to a cultivated hybrid.
– **Co-evolution**	mutual evolutionary convergence between different species.
– **Column or gynostemium**	(columnar) part of the flower where the female (stigma) and male (pollinia) sexual organs are attached.
– **Cross-pollination**	pollination of a flower with pollen delivered by another plant.
– **Epiphyte**	non-parasitic plant naturally occurring in trees.
– **Euglossine bees**	bees from Central and South America that usually have metallic colouring.
– **Lip or labellum**	one of the six petals of an orchid flower that is different from the other petals in size, form and/or colour.
– **Mimicry**	imitation of other plants and or animals.
– **Nectar**	sweet liquid secreted by some flowers to attract pollinators.
– **Nectar guides**	patterns visible in flowers that guide pollinators to the nectar and pollen.
– **Petals**	leaf-like structures in the flower.
– **Pollen**	fine to coarse powder (pollen grains) produced by the male parts of the flower, and used for pollination.
– **Pollination**	the transfer of pollen to the female reproductive structure, resulting into seed production when succesful.
– **Pollinia**	pollen bundles or aggregations of pollen attached to a band of tissue.
– **Pseudobulb**	a thickened stem that serves as storage organ for the plant.
– **Pseudocopulation**	attempt by male insects to mate with flowers they mistakenly think are females of their species.
– **Self-pollination**	pollination of a flower by its own pollen.
– **Spur**	tubular part of a flower with a closed tip usually filled with nectar.
– **Terrestrial**	plant that grows in the ground.

Literature

- **Anonymous, Musée International de la Parfumerie, Grasse. 1993.** *Vanilles et orchidées.* Editions Edisud, Aix-en-Provence, France.
- **Balis J. & Lawalrée A. 1961.** *L'orchidée en Belgique.* Catalogue n° 5, Bibliothèque Albert I, Bruxelles.
- **Blanco M.A. & Barboza G. 2005.** *Pseudocopulatory pollination in Lepanthes (Orchidaceae : Pleurothallidinae) by fungus gnats.* Annals of Botany 95: 763-772.
- **Boyle F. 1893.** *About Orchids, A Chat.* Chapman and Hall, London, UK.
- **Braem G. 1988.** *Paphiopedilum,* a monograph of all tropical and subtropical Asiatic slipper-orchids. Brücke Verlag Kurt Schmersow, Hildesheim, 249 pp.
- **Buchmann S.L. & G. P. Nabhan. 1996.** *The forgotten pollinators.* Island Press, Shearwater Books. Washington D.C./ Covelo, California, 292 pp.
- **Cogniaux A. 1896-1907.** *Dictionnaire iconographique des orchidées.* Dessins et aquarelles par Alphonse Goossens.
- **Cribb P.** *The Genus Paphiopedilum.* Royal Botanic Gardens, Kew, United Kingdom.
- **Dressler R.L. 1981.** *The orchids.* Natural history and classification. Cambridge, Massachusetts: Harvard University Press.
- **Endress P.K. 1994.** *Diversity and evolutionary biology of tropical flowers.* Cambridge University Press.
- **Fanfani A. 1989.** *The MacDonald's encyclopedia of orchids.* MacDonalds & Co, London, UK.
- **Garcia – Calderon y Ponce A. L. 2001.** *Orquideas metafisicas, comedia dramatica en cuatro actos.* Malaga, Espana.
- **Graham S. 2001.** *Illegal trade threatens African orchids.* Scientific American, 2 August 2001.
- **Grove D.L. 1995.** *Vandas and Ascocendas, and their combinations with other genera.* Timber Press, Portland, Oregon, 241 pp.
- **Hansen E. 2000.** *Orchideeënkoorts. Een verhaal over liefde, wellust en merkwaardige mensen.* Uitgeverij BZZTôH, 's Gravenhage, Nederland.
- **Hoffman Lewis M.W. 1990.** *Power and passion: the orchid in literature.* In: Arditti J. (Ed.) Orchid Biology: reviews and perspectives V: 207-250 pp.
- **Kaiser R. 1993.** *The scent of orchids. Olfactory and chemical investigations.* Editiones Roche, Basel, 259 pp.
- **Kaiser R. 2006.** *Flowers and fungi use scents to mimic each other.* Science 311: 806-807 pp.
- **Marinelli J. 2004.** *Plant: the ultimate visual reference to plants and flowers of the world.* Dorling Kindersley Limited, London.
- **Martinez Lopez R. 2006.** *Orquideas y mandalas – la sanacion cuantica del universo.* Ed. Vision Net, Madrid.
- **Micheneau C., Fournel J. & Pailler T. 2006.** *Bird pollination in an Angraecoid Orchid on Reunion Island* (Mascarene Archipelago, Indian Ocean). Annals of Botany 97(6): 965-974 pp.
- **Roguenant A., Raynal-Roques A. & Sell Y. 2005.** *Un amour d'orchidée. Le mariage de la fleur et de l'insecte.* Editions Belin.
- **Runkle E., Wang Y-T., Blanchard M. & Lopez R. 2006.** *Growing the best Phalaenopsis.* Part 1 : an introduction to potted Phalaenopsis orchids. Orchids 1 : 24-29 pp.
- **Schiestl F.P, Peakall R, Mant J.M, Ibarra F, Schulze C, Franke S. & Francke W. 2003.** *The chemistry of sexual deception in an orchid-wasp pollination system.* Science 302: 437-438 pp.
- **Thomas J. & Hess H. 1986.** *Orchid art and the orchid isle.* Malama Arts Inc., Honolulu, Hawaii, second printing.
- **Van der Pijl L. & Dodson C.H. 1966.** *Orchid flowers – their pollination and evolution.* University of Miami Press, Coral Gables, Florida, 214 pp.
- **Van der Cingel N.A. 1995.** *An atlas of orchid pollination: European orchids.* A.A. Balkema, Rotterdam / Brookfield, 175 pp.
- **Van der Cingel N.A. 2001.** *An atlas of orchid pollination: America, Africa, Asia and Australia.* A.A. Balkema, Rotterdam / Brookfield, 296 pp.
- **Vogel S. 1978.** *Pilzmückenblumen als Pilzmimeten.* Flora 167: 329-398 pp.
- **Wood J.J., Beaman R.S. & Beaman J.H. 1993.** *The plants of Mount Kinabalu 2.* Orchids. Royal Botanic Gardens, Kew.

About the author

Dr Anne Ronse (°1961) has been a plant lover since her childhood and developed a special interest in orchids from 1976 on. In 1984 she obtained a degree of Master in Agronomy at the University of Leuven (K.U. Leuven) and in 1993 she got a PhD in Applied Biological Sciences at the same university. Since 1988 Anne Ronse has been working as a researcher at the National Botanical Garden of Belgium (Meise) where she currently leads a research project on conservation biology of endangered plant species. Until the beginning of 2008 she has been president of the 'Brabantse Orchideeën Vereniging', one of Belgium's orchid societies, and organized several international orchid exhibitions.

Acknowledgements

I kindly thank the following people for graciously providing plants for the photographs in this book:
Diane and Dirk Bruyninckx (Akerne), Jacky and Willy Coeck (Jacky Orchids), Jan Moors (Crustacare) and Jan and Maggy Van Haute (Cymbiflor).

Author

Dr Anne Ronse

Photography

Bart Van Leuven
Tom Swijns
Justin Brown (p. 100-103)

Translation

X-L-Ent nv, Roeselare (BE)

Final Editing

Katrien Van Moerbeke

Layout and Print

Group Van Damme bvba, Oostkamp (BE)

Published by

Stichting Kunstboek bvba
Legeweg 165
B-8020 Oostkamp
Tel. +32 50 46 19 10
Fax +32 50 46 19 18
info@stichtingkunstboek.com
www.stichtingkunstboek.com

ISBN 978-90-5856-252-4
D/2008/6407/18
NUR 421